What Is A Canadian Literature?

What Is A Canadian Literature?

JOHN METCALF

Red Kite Press
Guelph, Ontario

Canadian Cataloguing in Publication Data

Metcalf, John, 1938-
    What is a Canadian literature?

Bibliography: p.
ISBN 0-920493-06-8 (bound). – ISBN 0-920493-05-X (pbk.)
ISBN 0-920493-07-6 (limited ed.)

1. Canadian literature (English) – 20th century –
History and criticism.* 2. Authors, Canadian
(English) – 20th century.* 1. Title.

PS 8071.4.M39 1988   C810'.9'0054   C88-095256-3
PR9189.6.M49 1988

Published by Red Kite Press, P.O. Box 30, Guelph, Ontario,
Canada N1H 6J6.

Printed and bound by The Porcupine's Quill, Inc. (Erin) in
November 1988. Typeset by The Coach House Press
(Toronto). The type is Ehrhardt and the stock is Zephyr
Antique Laid.

Red Kite Press logo is after a wood engraving
by G. Brender à Brandis.

For the paperback issue, the cover art is after a painting,
"Imagin," by Andrea Bolley.

For
DAVID COLBERT
original and *fierce*

One

IN 1982 I PUBLISHED a collection of essays and literary memoirs called *Kicking Against the Pricks*. In these essays I advanced with perfectly innocent intent four main claims. These were:

A) That successive Canadian governments have subsidized the arts in the hope that they will shape and define a national identity. That this pervasive identification of art with nationalism is pernicious and stands in the way of artistic and critical maturity.

B) That 'modernism' in fiction did not really arrive in Canada until, roughly speaking, the publication of Hugh Hood's story collection *Flying a Red Kite* in 1962. That the prose written in Canada prior to this – apart from a few isolated and atypical examples – was grimly bad then and is now unbearable.

C) That fiction in Canada had, therefore, no native tradition on which to draw and that the explosion in Canadian writing in the 1960s inevitably drew on the tradition of international modernism – a tradition which was by then some forty years old.

D) That most of the best writing in Canada since the early 1960s has been in the story form. That the emphasis has shifted from 'story-as-thing-to-be-understood' to 'story-as-thing-to-be-experienced', 'story-as-performance'. That to be able to understand stories in this way, the reader has to be more aware of style – of technique and rhetoric.

These points – with a few jollities thrown in by way of amplification and example – seemed to me simple and reasonably unexceptionable so I was rather surprised by some of the epithets that came my way in reviews – petty, vindictive, vitriolic, vain, poisonous, pathological, élitist, snob, and – to cap it all – Englishman.

The most recent reactions to *Kicking Against the Pricks* have come from Professor Sam Solecki of the University of Toronto. In an ambiguously titled piece "Some Kicks Against the Prick: John Metcalf in His Essays," which I courteously, and perhaps masochistically, accepted as a contribution to *The Bumper Book* (1986), Professor Solecki writes:

> Metcalf's problematic relationship to literary tradition seems to me to underlie, in part, his emphasis on style and on a criticism that focuses almost exclusively on style, form, and rhetoric. One of the more obvious consequences of a predominantly "practical" or textual or rhetorical criticism is that it eliminates most, perhaps all, of the distinctions that would allow us to discuss texts either historically or within national traditions. Approached in this way all literature is extra-territorial. The only basis on which a group of books could then be classified as English or Canadian or Australian would be political or geographical. (Obviously the argument would take a different form if we were dealing with a literature like Czech or French that is defined *a priori* by a unique language.) I'm not suggesting, however, that a content-oriented or thematic criticism is the alternative – that way lie Moss and madness. I simply want to make it clear that if we follow some of Metcalf's suggestions or those of critics who tempt us with Barthian *jouissance* or Derridean deconstruction then we are pulling the theoretical rug out from under Canadian studies constituted as a separate branch of English studies. That may or may not be a bad thing. If nothing else it would force us to re-examine more closely what our actual field of study is and how it relates to other areas of the discipline. But if we agree that our major texts – those which constitute or determine our field of study – are written in a modern or international style and if we take it for granted that "il n'y a pas de hors-texte" then we have no theoretical basis on which to constitute a canon that is specifically Canadian – unless we want to do it

on the basis of place of publication. We may agree with Metcalf's figure that "Canadian writing is only a weak current in a strong English-language river" ... but if we follow his argument we will have no way of distinguishing the one from the other.

Similarly, in dismissing "most Canadian writing up until 1950" as "rubbish" ... and by characterizing the best work of the past twenty-five years as modern or international in style Metcalf, consciously or unconsciously, leaves the Canadian writer and critic without a Canadian tradition.

What *is* this Canadian tradition of which Professor Solecki speaks?

Discussion about it has been going on since Confederation but its shape and outline remain vague and tenuous. Different critics seem to describe different traditions: John Sutherland's vision of the Canadian tradition is not A.J.M. Smith's; Margaret Atwood's tradition is not Robin Mathews'; T.D. MacLulich's sense of what should be valued differs radically from Ronald Sutherland's. The few texts we have are positively *beset* by theory.

The pros and cons of a Canadian literature have been dancing the same ritual dance for close to a hundred years: parochial against universal, nationalist against internationalist, sturdy modest Canadian against smarmy cosmopolitan with brilliantined hair. It is all rather tedious. And none of it, of course, has much to do with literature. In all these debates, the real subject is the politics of Canadian sovereignty.

What is distinctively Canadian in a Canadian literature? Which works should be enshrined in the Canadian canon? Which excluded? Who is a Canadian? Who not?

'Canadian-ness'.

'Canadian-ness' rather than quality has always been the Canadian concern.

Not much has changed in the last forty years; one still hears in 1987 the same dreary tunes one heard in 1947. In 1947 John

Sutherland in his introduction to *Other Canadians* quoted from a Canadian Authors' Association review of Patrick Anderson's *A Tent for April*:

"His verse contains many ideas which are essentially Canadian, and that is good, for he may stimulate other Canadian poets to choose their homeland as subject for their verse. If this is accomplished Mr. Anderson will have made a valuable contribution to Canadian literature."

In 1987 in *Quill & Quire* a review of an anthology of Canadian novellas said in its opening paragraph: "... of the seven collected authors, five are immigrants, one is an expatriate, and only one, Keath Fraser, is a native-born, resident Canadian."

Two influential attempts at describing and defining Canadian literature have been Margaret Atwood's *Survival* (1972) and Robin Mathews' *Canadian Literature: Surrender or Revolution* (1978).

Survival is a jolly and vigorous call to arms. Margaret Atwood's abstracting and moralizing mind draws generalities from the texts and constructs patterns. Canadian literature, we discover, reveals us as Victims. We are Position One Victims, Position Two Victims, or Position Three Victims. We can't become Creative Non-Victims – the desirable Position Four – until we have changed society. We can change society by buying back our economy from the Americans, by politically restructuring ourselves, and by changing the way we think and feel about ourselves.

The book is suffused with radical innocence.

Because Margaret Atwood is using literature to illustrate the thesis that Canada is an oppressed colony, that it is, in fact, a Victim, she does not attempt to evaluate the books she discusses. She is not setting out to select and describe Canada's best writing. But because her subject is 'Canadian-ness', she is, willy-nilly, writing an account of those books which she feels should be of central interest to Canadians. In other words, although it is not her primary intention, she *is* defining what she feels to be Canada's central tradition.

Some Canadian writers do not fit the theory. Margaret Atwood herself in "Mathews and Misrepresentation," an essay published in *This Magazine* in 1973 and republished in her book *Second Words* (1982), comments on her neglect of George Jonas, Michael Ondaatje, Malcolm Lowry, and Brian Moore. She says: "It seems to me dangerous to talk about 'Canadian' patterns of sensibility in the work of people who entered and / or entered-and-left the country at a developmentally late stage of their lives."

The connections of Lowry and Moore to Canada are matters open to debate – though Moore holds Canadian citizenship – but Ondaatje? He arrived here at a developmentally late stage in his life, certainly. But what is he? Not Dutch. Not Sri Lankan. Not British. He has lived in Canada for a long time. He is a Canadian citizen. He has written all his work here. He writes in English, one of Canada's official languages. He has been a vital part of literary life in Canada for years. He has twice been honoured with Canada's highest literary award. Sam Solecki has edited a big fat book about him. I'd tend to think of him as a Canadian.

Why is Susanna Moodie, an Englishwoman who arrived here at a developmentally late stage, central to CanLit?

Why is Frederick Philip Grove, an ex-German bigamist, a central part of the Canadian tradition if Ondaatje isn't?

Is Margaret Atwood implying that all pigs are equal but some pigs are more equal than others? Is she implying that the tradition is now closed, that the literature has ended? That immigrants need not apply? Is 'Canadian-ness' now only the property of those whom Robin Mathews calls 'birthright Canadians'?

If Ondaatje must be pushed to the periphery or considered in some special kind of light, where does that leave Leon Rooke, Audrey Thomas, Janette Turner Hospital, Paulette Jiles, Kent Thompson, J. Michael Yates, Michael Bullock, John Mills, George McWhirter, Carol Shields, Clark Blaise, Austin Clarke,

Rohinton Mistry... all citizens, and all, to the best of my knowledge, scribbling away.

W.H. New writes in *Dreams of Speech and Violence: The Art of the Short Story in Canada and New Zealand* (1987):

> It would be easy to invent a category, 'immigrant writing' and let it contain all such writers: Kreisel, Lowry, Pacey; British-born John Metcalf; US-born Audrey Thomas, Clark Blaise, Kent Thompson, Leon Rooke, Ann Copeland, Susan Kerslake, Elizabeth Spencer, Jane Rule; Kenya-born Bill Schermbrucker; Australia-born Daphne Marlatt; Malta-born Seán Virgo; Barbados-born Austin Clarke; Trinidad-born Sam Selvon; and others with backgrounds in Italy, Germany, India, Chile, Guyana, China, and Japan. Yet to do so would be implicitly to find a way of excluding them from the mainstream, of defining them as a group called 'other' to be consequently held apart. And while it would be blind to deny that some Canadians would regard this as a proper attitude to take, it has in fact been more characteristic of Canadian experience to make the otherness its own.

My own experiences as a 'non-birthright' Canadian and my general sense of the way our literature is received would tend to make me think of Bill New's last sentence as pious or ingenuous.

Who *should* be counted?

In "Notes of a Natural Son," an essay published in *The Bumper Book*, John Mills comments on a conference on the Canadian novel that he attended some years earlier:

> Margaret Atwood was one of the panelists, along with Sylvia Fraser, Robert Kroetsch, Harold Horwood, and Audrey Thomas. In some significant respects this group could hardly be more representative of the problem of "whom to count," for Robert Kroetsch was born in Canada but, at the time of the conference, was living in Binghamton, New

York, while Audrey Thomas, born and raised in Binghamton, New York, had lived for many years in Vancouver, BC, and Harold Horwood, as a middle-aged Newfoundlander, was evidently neither born a Canadian nor did he become one by chosen act, but was created one by government fiat in 1949.

Would it be mischievous at this point to suggest that traditions themselves change course? That in twenty years some of these 'peripheral' writers will be seen as mainstays of some more freshly minted version of the tradition? Would it be mischievous to recall that the course of British poetry was changed radically by the arrival in England of Ezra Pound and T.S. Eliot, two Americans both at a developmentally late stage?

Most of the theories about our literature are both comic and distasteful. It is not an elevating spectacle to see the wagons drawn into a circle with the guns blazing inwards. The only thing most of our critics have in common is the desire to exclude. Theories about Canadian literature tend to reflect the larger social attitudes and nearly all the visions of our literature are nationalistic, chauvinistic, smug, and amazingly *white*.

Outside the laager, the unheeded natives are getting restless. Some of our myopic critics might do well to note that the latest census statistics record that 'ethnics' – those 'peripheral' ethnics – now constitute 33% of the population and that forecasts suggest that within six years the 'ethnics' will outnumber the English and the French combined.

There are very few brilliant writers in Canada; an addition to their ranks would have a great impact on the way we thought about Canadian writing. The advent of *one* brilliant new writer would force us to reshuffle the pack and establish a different ranking. Imagine the advent of a new writer as hugely gifted as Alice Munro.

But now imagine that this writer is of Chinese origins or West or East Indian and that his or her writing reflects not only immigrant experience in Canada but Vietnam or India or Trinidad.

Imagine that from those Canadian communities we choose to call 'ethnic' (i.e. Canadians who aren't *really* Canadians) emerges a Timothy Mo, an Anita Desai, a V.S. or Shiva Naipaul, an R.K. Narayan, or a Robert Hayden.

Imagine now the emergence of *five* such writers.

What would *this* do to our sense of Canada, to our sense of Canadian writing, to our tradition?

Two

ALTHOUGH SOME OF US might be slightly daunted by the complexities of defining 'Canadian-ness', Robin Mathews is not. In his astounding book *Canadian Literature: Surrender or Revolution* – a vaguely Marxist mishmash of gathered articles and essays – Mathews advances the idea that what differentiates true Canadian writing from American writing is that American writing celebrates liberal anarchist individualism whereas Canadian writing in the *true* tradition, the non-Atwoodian tradition, celebrates collectivity and community.

The Canadian tradition in fiction started, according to Mathews, in 1832 with John Richardson's *Wacousta*.

"*Wacousta*," writes Mathews, "is the first novel in a tradition which declares that Canadians have within their identity and imagination a strong consciousness of collective existence and solidarity, and the possibility of new political forms that can grow out of it."

If you received the impression that that sentence sounded a bit odd and didn't quite seem somehow to make sense, you'd probably be right. Even brief exposure to Mathews induces that stunned and buzzing sensation usually associated with the third martini.

In Mathews' version of CanLit, Hugh MacLennan is a Canadian writer but Mordecai Richler is not. Nor is Irving Layton. Nor is Morley Callaghan. Callaghan is in fact a traitor to 'Canadian-ness' because he openly admits to having embraced the influence of Ernest Hemingway. Then, too, Callaghan is a Roman Catholic. As was Hemingway. And as Mathews remarks, the Roman Catholic Church, like the multinational corporations, has always denied the relevance of national boundaries.

Mathews on poetry is equally penetrating.

It goes something like this: England was an imperial power but unlike the Americans was a *good* imperial power because the British and the Canadians had a vision of Canadian evolution towards equality and independence. The Confederation Poets wrote within the British Victorian tradition but were adding to that tradition landscape details which were distinctively Canadian.

(I assume he means such things as: 'the scarlet of the maples', 'crimson forest', 'sumachs on the hills' turning 'their green to red', 'a line of grey snake-fence', cattle gazing 'with longing through the grey, mossed rails' – all good and new and necessary stuff but scarcely rivetting.)

After the Confederation Poets peter out, there seems to be a gap in the Mathews account until the 1940s arrive and the British-Canadian tradition is destroyed by influences from the USA imported by traitors at McGill University – such anti-Canadian renegades as A.J.M. Smith, Frank Scott, Louis Dudek, Irving Layton, and P.K. Page. The Evil American Empire further triumphed in its destruction of a native Canadian voice when Raymond Souster championed Charles Olson and when George Bowering and Frank Davey founded what Mathews calls The Black Mountain Imitation School.

By the time Mathews has finished winnowing the wheat from the liberal, anarchist, individualistic, capitalist, bourgeois chaff, there's not enough grain in the pail to cover the back of your hand.

And we are no closer to defining a Canadian literature.

GEORGE BOWERING DESCRIBES the Canadian Tradition in literature as a *chimera*. He claims that snowdrifts have very little to do with *him*; they're not a feature of the Okanagan Valley. In his marvellously titled book of literary criticism *Craft Slices* (1985), he writes of his student days:

> We had always found the Okanagan Valley, which extended southward almost to Wenatchee, Washington, more a fact than the forty-ninth parallel.
>
> At the University of British Columbia, ... [we] young poets who had come down from the hills ... felt that the desert valley kids shared an ethogeography that fed our

imaginations in a way that Creative Writing 102, with its chimera of a "Canadian Tradition" never could....

... I did not study CanLit formally, and had to do my learning while writing. But the more I learned, the more I was confused by the applause of the patriotic CanLit professors, who, eager for a long tradition and therefore a significant area of study to make their jobs meaningful to the eyes of outsiders, would support writers from the past who, on the evidence of their writing, had more to offer to sociology than to literature. When I first saw the works of the "Confederation Poets," I thought that they were poets composing around the time of Confederation; but I found out to my surprise that they were born about then. Their poems, it seems to me, are largely less apt imitations of Wordsworth a century earlier.

With its large landmass and small and recent population, Canada has had to endure a lot of (and late) content-oriented writing. We still get it, especially as it is celebrated by our professors, who still operate as thematic critics, counting the number of times the maple leaf appears in our poems, or snow in our fictions....

Since 1946, Canadian poets, and since 1970, Canadian fiction writers, have caught up with the postmodern world; but the purveyors of Canadian culture, the reviewers, professors and such like, are still promoting work that looks as if it would be comfortable in a Georgian drawing-room.

And in a recent letter to me, George Bowering writes:

I am probably as much confused as you are about the meanings of the phrase "The Canadian Tradition." As you will know, I generally use the phrase as a joke, with a kind of superior sneer on my thin Protestant lips. I have noted for some time that Mathews and the acolytes he amazingly gets around him never bother to define the term.

... As a Canadian, let us say, it bothers me that the pieces of literature generally picked up by those National Socialist literati and championed as the Canadian Tradition are almost without exception 12th-rate writing, amateur grundge, imitative of some inferior English dribble of a previous time....

As a westerner, too, of course, I am colonized by the dinks who identify the Canadian Tradition with some inferior writing done in Ontario and Quebec and maybe New Brunswick. If we [and here Bowering means writers in BC], responding to our own situation, do not write like a snow-fearing Anglo-hick, we are accused of being something foreign.

Is Bowering merely eccentric in his assertion that the Canadian Tradition is a *chimera*?
Consider this.
At a recent conference in Venice entitled "Cross-Currents in Commonwealth Literature," Ray Smith gave a paper in which he said:

... there is something illusory about Canada, something fuzzy, foggy, undefinable. There is, first of all, so much of it that it is impossible to know all its parts. What seems reasonable to an Anglo-Quebecer – that bilingualism is a necessary fact of life – becomes, on the prairies, fascist lunacy....

More profoundly, critics have developed two competing families of modern Canadian fiction. The eastern one has Callaghan and MacLennan as patriarchs and marks the beginning of the modern era with Hugh Hood's *Flying a Red Kite*, with the line of descent through Munro, Laurence, Metcalf, Blaise, Atwood, and so on, with sometime emigrant influences from Gallant, Levine, and Richler. This is primarily a sophisticated urban literature. The western line runs from Grove, Sinclair Ross, and W.O. Mitchell, and marks the beginning of the modern era with Sheila Watson or Margaret Laurence, then on powerfully, inevitably, to Wiebe, Kroetsch, and their followers. This prairie family is rural: it begins with the land, populates it with native people, then with immigrants. The two families are not entirely mutually exclusive – Margaret Laurence is admitted to both – but are nearly so. While I was serving as writer-in-residence at the University of Alberta, Edmonton, last winter, a critic whom I personally respect explained the prairie family to me, adding that it was clearly canonical and all Canadian fiction not of the prairie model is marginal. Both families ignore Newfoundland, the Maritimes, and British Columbia.

Smith restricts his remarks to fiction but the situation with poetry is even more extreme. The critic Dennis Cooley, himself a prairie poet, writing in *The Vernacular Muse: The Eye and Ear in Contemporary Literature* (1987), advances the claim that poetry from the prairies is marked by a 'prairie vernacular', *a distinctive regional language* which is a demotic Western reaction to the élitist language of the oppressive East – an odd assertion in many ways, given that most prairie poets seem to be tenured academics. But the feelings of division are deep and real.

The respected Quebec-based critic Ronald Sutherland presents yet another divergent view of the Canadian Tradition. He would exclude: Adele Wiseman, Sinclair Ross, Robertson Davies, W.O. Mitchell, Alice Munro, Morley Callaghan, and Stephen Leacock. In an essay from *The New Hero* (1977) called "The Mainstream," a piece marked by implacable Gallic logic, Sutherland writes:

... a sphere of consciousness which is uniquely Canadian does exist in this country, and from within this sphere the mainstream of Canadian literature is rapidly emerging.

The distinguishing feature of the sphere of consciousness which governs the mainstream of Canadian literature is, understandably enough, the same feature which principally distinguishes the Canadian nation – the co-existence in this country of two major ethnic or language groups....

May I repeat once again that the mainstream of Canadian literature has nothing to do with literary merit; it is a matter of sphere of consciousness, an author's awareness of and sensitivity to fundamental aspects of both major language groups in Canada, and of the inter-relationships between these two groups. Now I know that the idea of a mainstream bothers some writers and critics, who seem to presume that it is akin to the Order of Canada or whatever it is that the government put into operation to celebrate the centennial, inanely proclaiming certain writers first-class, others second-class, and the rest beneath classification. In fact, however, the mainstream concept is a thematic identification and not a value judgement. There is no need for a writer to be in the mainstream in order to achieve literary quality, as indeed many of the Canadian writers of merit are not. Adele Wiseman, Sinclair Ross, Robertson Davies, W.O. Mitchell, Louis Hémon, Alice Munro, Morley Callaghan, and Stephen Leacock are obvious examples. But that there must be a mainstream, however, is to me a matter of syllogistic logic, for as I will further elaborate below, in order to have a Canadian literature it is necessary to have a Canadian nation, and the survival of the Canadian nation presupposes a *modus vivendi* between the nation's two major language groups....

At one time, only a few years ago in fact, Hugh MacLennan appeared almost the only modern, major creative writer in Canada who was moving with the mainstream current. Certain authors of the past – political writers, commentators, journalists – had been swept up, but not major creative writers. A few writers in each language group, of course, had indicated a superficial awareness of the other.... But in recent years, several Canadian authors have been drawn into the mainstream, have developed much more than a superficial awareness. Hugh Hood, both in his novels and his stories, is one example. James Bacque in the novel *Big Lonely,* Leonard Cohen in *Beautiful Losers,* Ralph Gustafson in his recent poetry, Dave Godfrey both explicitly and symbolically, Margaret Atwood in *Survival....*

This passage repays several readings. It should fill the thoughtful reader with mirthful unease.

Big Lonely?

This tenured twaddle is more than dotty; it is *exaltedly* dotty.

Canadian literature, then, is not a commonly-agreed-upon corpus of work. There exists no consensus. We cannot even agree about who our best writers are. There exists no hierarchy. Criticism is in the hands of rabid factions. There exists no single critical work which offers an undisputed overview. The readership is seemingly far too small to apply to all these problems the brake of common sense.

IF OUR OWN VIEW of our literature is obscured by rifts, feuds, jealousies, geography, and doctrinal controversy, is the view any clearer to those outside? Even to ask this question is embarrassing. Canadian literature simply does not exist for American or British readers. Individual writers are known – principally to academics – but there seems little sense that they come from a tradition and a national literature.

In explanation of this, Mathews advances the Evil Empire theory. He writes:

> Imperialist countries – which control the publishing, the reading, the forms of thought of other communities – usually have the classics they produce hailed immediately as 'international'. Empires exert what Harold Innis called 'monopolies of knowledge'. The monopolies of knowledge that empires possess make possible the dominance of their ideologies and ideas. The classics that the imperial power produces are believed to be central and significant in the world.... An imperial country can impose its ideas of cen-

trality and cultural significance on other countries to the extent that it has political or economic power over them. A genius in an imperial country is described as an "international" genius....

When we turn to look at some of the classics in Canadian literature, we bump against the old problems – and some new ones. The genius of Canada, the expression which is most characteristic of the society itself, is hard for many people to grasp, to understand. The voice of a colonial culture is hard to hear. And there are many, always, who don't want to hear it. The spokesmen for literature in Canada, until recently, have been trained in the literary genius of the English language, which means they have read deeply and widely in the classics, the comments upon the classics, and the literature peripheral to the classics of Britain and the United States. They have not read deeply and widely in the classics of Canada.... But Canadian genius and the Canadian voice cannot be suppressed forever.

Another stirring call to arms! What Mathews has to say here even contains a hint of truth. The United States *isn't* deeply interested in Canada. It is doubtless true that the power and centrality of a country in world affairs *does* affect the importance granted to that country's literature. But *has* the United States suppressed the Canadian genius and the Canadian voice?

Well, we're certainly awash in American books and TV programmes. But no one forced them on us at gunpoint. And that's a central argument to make; cultural nationalists always seem to assume that Canadians are totally passive, that 'Canada' is a limp unconscious body upon which any ravisher can work his will. Might one suggest that we haven't a clearly visible literature *because we haven't wanted one enough?*

We can't *legislate* one. We can't entrench one by establishing quotas. We can only establish a literature through wanting one *enough* and this has nothing to do with governments and trade practices and ownership of the means of production and distribution. Nor does it have anything to do with being Canadian.

It must be very *comforting* to be able to believe the things Mathews believes, but the facts are awkward ... When one descends from windy and rhetorical generalities to gritty particulars, the truth seems otherwise. Far from suppressing the Canadian voice, the United States seems to have broadcast it.

Most of our famed 'Confederation Poets' regularly published their work in the United States rather than in Canada; their Toronto was Boston. The awful Bliss Carman lived most of his life in Connecticut. Many of the better-known Canadian writers sought and found publication in the USA: Charles Sangster, Charles G.D. Roberts, Bliss Carman, Sara Jeannette Duncan, Archibald Lampman, Duncan Campbell Scott, Lucy Maud Montgomery, Mazo de la Roche, Frederick Philip Grove, E.J. Pratt, Raymond Knister, Morley Callaghan, Sinclair Ross, Ernest Buckler, A.M. Klein ...

Americans may not be particularly interested in Canadian literature but they don't seem averse to books by individual Canadians. They seem quite content to publish Ralph Gustafson, Irving Layton, Robertson Davies, Margaret Avison, Mavis Gallant, Margaret Laurence, Mordecai Richler, Alice Munro, Marian Engel, Margaret Atwood, Michael Ondaatje – the list is long and growing.

Margaret Atwood has even become a heroine of American *popular* culture – having been voted by a popular American magazine Woman of the Year, an honour she shared with two fictional policewomen from the TV show *Cagney and Lacey,* one of whom is alcoholic and one of whom isn't, and with the enormously endowed country-and-western singer Dolly Parton.

Would Robin Mathews describe *this* as the suppression of Canadian genius?

Would it be mischievous to suggest that the Americans and the British seem to be blind to Canadian literature because Canadian literature is rather difficult to see? Would it be mischievous to suggest that Canadian literature is something of a fabrication? That its alleged hoary antiquity (*Wacousta,* for God's sake!) is academic naughtiness and desperate invention? That the simple fact is that there haven't yet been many Canadian literary texts of high quality? That, in fact, the Americans now tend to publish *most* of the books which achieve acclaim in Canada?

Before taking final and grateful leave of Robin Mathews, it's probably important to glance at his 'if you aren't one of us, you can't understand or criticize us' argument. This meretricious argument explains why Canadian literature is not visible to readers and critics in England or the USA. It's an argument that seems to hold great appeal for the insecure and for those suffering from feelings of inferiority and over the last few years it has been advanced by such varied special interest groups as militant blacks, militant homosexuals, militant women, and white South Africans.

Mathews trundles this one out against W.J. Keith of the University of Toronto for having criticized Charles G.D. Roberts and for having found him wanting when compared with his contemporaries in England and America. Mathews writes:

> The critics ... are frequently immigrants to Canada, having received most of their education abroad, and having spent their formative years in another culture, a metropolitan culture. They are not usually specialists in Canadian literature. Their criticism arises from their claims to understanding about the universal truth of art, which usually means their limited experience with British or US literature. And since Canadian literature is parochial, anyone can write about it. The kind of critic in question considers Canadian effort, always, overpraised. He seeks to introduce 'objective and discriminating appraisal'. By that he means a number of things:
>
> 1) The artist is to be compared to artists of a totally different community and culture.
> 2) The artist is not to be allowed the possibility of speaking a tongue unfamiliar to metropolitan ears.
> 3) He is to be measured against 'the great writers'.

4) He is not to be compared to the artists of his own country.

5) His themes and concerns are not to be related to the themes and concerns of his own country.

That is how we get 'objective and discriminating criticism'. The critic who doesn't know what the Canadian imagination is about, what Canadian art is about, analyses Canadian art against art that is about something else. The antelope, in that critic's eyes, is considered a grotesque donkey. The Canadian artist is read out of context and, if necessary, is forced out of context to make him measurable against the alien artist.

It's difficult to know where first to tackle this demagogic farrago so I'll examine it briefly in the order Mathews presents it.

1) *Critics from outside Canada have a low or misguided opinion of Canadian writing because they insist on comparing Canadian artists with "artists of a totally different community and culture."*

Mathews here is trying to suggest that comparing a Canadian poem with a British or American poem is as culturally inappropriate as comparing, say, an Hellenic statue and a Congolese fetish figure. He avoids the central point that artists in England, the USA, Canada, Australia, India, and South Africa *write in the same language.* They are of different social communities but they belong to precisely the same literary culture. In all those countries, a sonnet is a sonnet. There exists no such thing as an Australian sonnet.

2) *The critics will not read Canadian writing because they are unused to the language of Canadians. "The artist is not to be allowed the possibility of speaking a tongue unfamiliar to metropolitan ears."*

It is difficult to credit but Mathews *seems* to be suggesting here that there is a Canadian language or dialect. The effete, sophisticated metropolitans cannot understand us because we rougher but truer and more decent Canadians speak an unfamiliar language of our own. Mathews offers no examples.

All this is dreadfully specious stuff. Only sophisticated people read and write books in the first place. Books are not written by verbally weird Newfoundland cod-jiggers. And the metropolitan ear which adjusted itself to the later Henry James and the earlier William Faulkner can adjust itself to anything. Far from trying to silence tongues unfamiliar to metropolitan ears, it was the metropolitan Brits who joyfully seized upon and promoted the works of writers from the West Indies and West Africa, books employing in many cases distinct and unfamiliar dialects.

3) *The critics measure Canadian writers "against 'the great writers'."*

The words 'the great writers' are placed by Mathews in inverted commas implying that the great are not really great, implying that they're considered great merely because they hail from imperial countries. 'Greatness' is an uncomfortable idea for those who deal in CanLit but to shrink from comparative evaluation and to deny greatness is to embrace mediocrity. Which is precisely what *most* Canadian critics and commentators have done for the past fifteen years. Which is why we have to dig it all up and start again.

4) *The critics will not compare Canadian writers with other Canadian writers.*

This implies that if the 'foreign' critic *were* to do so, then things would be revealed or understood which international comparisons obscure. If you compare one dwarf with another dwarf, does that make the taller dwarf tall? This is merely a replay of Mathews' first point – that our artists are of a different community and culture. It is a replay of the 'if you aren't one of us, you can't understand or criticize us' argument. It is a lie.

5) *The critics will not relate a Canadian's themes and concerns to the themes and concerns of Canada.*

I'm not quite sure what Mathews means by this – as so often in his work. What *are* the themes and concerns of Canada? Few writers set out to write consciously about the concerns of their country unless the country is in crisis or in a state of revolution. Or unless they're engaged in propaganda. Such concerns might *emerge* in one way or another from the body of a writer's work but not in any theoretic or programmatic way. Most writers hymn, as Auden put it, the small and journal wonders. And how do the small and journal wonders relate to Free Trade, Regional Disparity, Native Rights, and Arctic Sovereignty?

Our only writer who *did* set out to write about Canadian concerns and wrote about them in a programmatic way – Hugh MacLennan – condemned his work by so doing to the fusty and eternal embrace of numberless Boards of Education.

In the deployment of these arguments, it's difficult to decide whether Mathews is being dishonest, demagogic, or is simply dim-witted. One final example may help in making that decision. What follows is from an essay on Sir Charles G.D. Roberts:

No serious Canadian writer is Wordsworthian, though he or she may have read Wordsworth. The writer may even have borrowed phrases from Wordsworth, subjects even. But in his or her best work the serious Canadian writer cannot be Wordsworthian. For a single reason. The leech gatherer, to say it bluntly, would be destroyed by climate in nine-tenths of Canada before one winter was well begun. Wordsworth's reality, in some of its most characteristic qualities, is alien in Canada.

It is sobering to remember – no! I won't descend to comic cliché – it is a *disgrace* that this knockabout Monty Python logic represents the considered literary responses of a full professor with tenure at one of our more respected institutions of higher learning. I *grieve* for the generation of students on whom Mathews inflicted in the name of Canadian literature such mindlessness and blinkered bad taste.

Three

NOW THAT WE'VE CIRCLED the elephant of CanLit and received the reports of the various blind investigators, perhaps it will be useful to return to the ideas from *Kicking Against the Pricks* which so disturbed Professor Solecki. I'd like to go through them and make a few comments which might help us descry CanLit's real shape.

The first idea was that there is in Canada a pervasive identification of art with nationalism and that this is pernicious and stands in the way of artistic and critical maturity.

The idea that literature should serve what is essentially a *political* function, the defining of the Canadian identity, is pervasive. It underlies most government thinking on the arts and is a concern of far too many critics. Intelligent critics and bureaucrats tend to wince when the idea is put baldly, so they disguise it with euphemisms. They talk of fiction and poetry as 'introducing us to ourselves and to each other'; of Canada's literary 'map'; of 'filling in the white spaces' on that map. But they're still talking about using literature to promote national identity and unity.

What a dreadful burden of self-consciousness for the Canadian writer and reader to drag around! Am I in this novel standing sufficiently on guard? Do writers in England, I wonder, sit down each day agonizing over how best they can manifest Britishness? Or Americans how they best can illustrate The American Way? Are British and American writers penalized if they set their fictions outside their respective national boundaries?

It's comic but true – sadly true – that Canadian writers who give their books non-Canadian settings are regarded by many reviewers as having committed treasonable acts.

A few years ago I published an anthology of stories by seven writers I considered the country's best. The book was called *Making It New*. There was an outcry from reviewers. Three of the seven writers had been born outside Canada and two had lived away from Canada for many years. Seven of the fourteen stories in the book were *set* outside Canada – one of them in Budapest, a location which seemed to particularly enrage one reviewer.

The Montreal *Gazette* headlined its review "Short and Sweet, but Hardly Canadian."

I.M. Owen in *Books in Canada* in a moaning review entitled, significantly, "To See Ourselves" said:

> But doesn't the reader in another country who buys or borrows a book of specifically Canadian stories want to learn from it something of what it's like to be Canadian?

Well, I.M. Owen, the answer to that is: I hope not.

If I were an intelligent reader in another country, I don't think I'd look to imaginary characters in a story for such information. Readers in another country would end up with an oddly skewed view of contemporary Quebec if, for example, they relied on the works of Marie-Claire Blais or Hubert Aquin. Most writers and most stories don't set out to convey what it's like to be Canadian. How *would* you convey it? What *is* it like? I wouldn't read a book of Brazilian stories to see what it was like to be Brazilian; I'd read it to see what pleasures good Brazilian practitioners of the form could give me. In other words, I read literature as literature and I don't use literature as sociology, history, anthropology, or travel guide.

The *point* of my quoting from these reviews is this: they reveal an emphasis and a criterion of criticism found only in Canada. 'Polish-born Joseph Conrad Sets New Novella in Congo.' No one in Canada remarks on this emphasis. It is profoundly anti-literary and militates against our achieving a literary culture of any sophistication.

Cultural nationalism comes in cycles in Canada. The strange thing is that, the enthusiasm over, nothing much is left behind. The wave crests, runs down, flattens, and the sea is level as before. Earlier flood periods of literary enthusiasm left little in the way of deposit – certainly not an audience. It seems that we have to start afresh each time. My own career has coincided with one of these cycles and I can report confidently that the enthusiasm was nearly always for some ill-defined nationalist vision and only rarely for a novel, a story, or a poem which had lodged itself in someone's heart.

The enthusiasm for The Group of Seven is an illustration of the same phenomenon. It was never a genuine enthusiasm for and engagement with *paint*. Had it been, our legacy today would be an active, informed audience. The reality is suggested by a remark made to me by the owner of one of Toronto's most prestigious galleries; she said that among her clients she has only seventeen private individuals who buy paintings.

Because the paintings of The Group of Seven were viewed not as paintings but as icons of 'Canadian-ness', painting in Canada is still seeking an audience. Exactly the same thing is true of our literature. We must stop viewing Hugh MacLennan, say, as an icon and instead we must start asking ourselves if his novels are good novels. And if we decide that they are not, we must have the courage to stop inflicting them on hapless students.

We cannot build a literature on a foundation of lies. We must stop presenting E.J. Pratt, that composer of forced and trivial epics, as a great Canadian poet. We must stop teaching students that *The Farm Show* and *On the Job* are plays worthy of their attention or that they are indeed *plays*. There are many reputations our heated cultural nationalists have boosted and inflated – and all need cast on them a cold and critical eye. There are many lies to which we have consented with our silence and we will have to repudiate every last one of them. Only by presenting to students the best of all literature in English can we rear up a generation with the necessary equipment to appreciate Canadian writing and to make it better by their informed critical responses as readers.

THE SECOND REMARK that upset Professor Solecki was that 'modernism' in fiction did not arrive in Canada until about 1962 and that most prose prior to this was bad then and is now unbearable.

I can't really see what's upsetting about this assertion. It seems to me incontestable. If Professor Solecki can name any 'modernist' novels and stories published in Canada prior to 1962 other than Sheila Watson's insufferably contrived *The Double Hook*, I'd appreciate the information. But perhaps it's the assertion that much of the prose is bad that disturbs him. He writes:

... in dismissing "most Canadian writing up until 1950" as "rubbish" ... and by characterizing the best work of the past twenty-five years as modern or international in style Metcalf, consciously or unconsciously, leaves the Canadian writer and critic without a Canadian tradition.

(Professor Solecki's use of the words "Canadian tradition" begs, as we have seen, many questions but I wish to postpone for a moment discussion of 'tradition' and 'modernism'.)

I would assert again that most prose fiction in Canada up to, say, 1962 was, at best, dreary. Most of Professor Solecki's 'Canadian tradition' is the handiwork of academic resurrection-men. Literary nationalism has boosted and bloated the reputations of such figures as John Richardson, Frederick Philip Grove, Morley Callaghan, Hugh MacLennan, Sinclair Ross, Ernest Buckler, and W.O. Mitchell. The academic CanLit establishment has stamped them as 'Classics'. They are, of course, nothing of the sort. Their books are, in the main, dull and flawed. They were old-fashioned when they were written and are now antiquated. Is to say this to deprive anybody of anything? Is to draw attention to their quite awful inadequacies of language to leave the Canadian writer and critic without a Canadian tradition? And if it is, does it matter? Who would wish to identify with a tradition of mediocre writing?

Never mind the Canadian writer and critic; what about the poor Canadian reader?

In their indecent haste to invent a tradition, the scholars have cemented these and even lesser writers into the curricula and reference books. The cement is hardening and if we don't dig it out *now* it will be too late. The process of canonization is picking up speed. The appetite grows by what it feeds on. Some literary nationalists can scarcely wait for the obsequies to end before indulging in hasty hagiography – witness the sloppy, sentimental treatment accorded the reputations of Marian Engel and Alden Nowlan.

Marian Engel wrote one good minor novel, *The Honeyman Festival* – a book I frequently recommend. She was a serious writer but she was not a major writer. Few of us are. Alden Nowlan was a writer who started strongly and declined in ability and taste as his reputation increased. I expressed this opinion once to a teacher of English in a university who replied that he didn't think it was an appropriate thing to say about a man who had cancer.

THE ASSERTION which most upset Professor Solecki was this:

That fiction in Canada had no native tradition on which to draw and that the explosion in Canadian writing in the 1960s inevitably drew on the tradition of international modernism – a tradition which was by then some forty years old.

It was of this assertion that Professor Solecki said:

... in dismissing "most Canadian writing up until 1950" as "rubbish" ... and by characterizing the best work of the past twenty-five years as modern or international in style Metcalf, consciously or unconsciously, leaves the Canadian writer and critic without a Canadian tradition.

He also wrote:

... if we agree that our major texts – those which constitute or determine our field of study – are written in a modern or international style ... then we have no theoretical basis on which to constitute a canon that is specifically Canadian –

unless we want to do it on the basis of place of publication.

It is important to put Professor Solecki's essay – and these quotations from it – into a context. The essay was printed in *The Bumper Book*, an anthology of contentious essays and squibs about Canadian writing edited by me and published in 1986. (I urge the entire thing upon you; it is doubtless unobtainable at most good bookstores but copies of the book and of its splendid successor, *Carry On Bumping*, may be had from the proprietors of ECW Press, 307 Coxwell Avenue, Toronto, Ontario, Canada M4L 3B5.) It was part of Professor Solecki's intention to paint me as, in his words, Canadian literature's "resident curmudgeon." He also asserts that my conscious or unconscious motivation for claiming

that most Canadian fiction prior to 1962 is glumly bad,

that most Canadian prose since that time has been in an international style,

that most of the best writing in Canada since the early 1960s has been in the story form,

is that I'm an immigrant to Canada and I don't fit into the Canadian tradition and I'm saying these things "to recast the Canadian tradition" in such a way that, as a writer of stories, I'll "have a place in it."

All this is, so far as I'm concerned, warfare of the most genial kind. But the opinions of curmudgeons are often taken to be cranky and eccentric and so I'd like to make clear that my claim that most writing in Canada since 1962 is international in style is not peculiar to me. It is a topic explored as early as 1967 in *The Modern Century* by the much-respected Northrop Frye. Frye states that there is an international style common to all industrialized democracies and that "Complete immersion in the international style is a primary cultural requirement, especially for countries whose cultural traditions have been formed since 1867, like ours."

That noted, let us return to the lists.

Professor Solecki's position doesn't seem to me to exhibit a firm logical grip. Does he mean to say that I'm wrong in characterizing the best work of the past twenty-five years as international in style? Presumably this *is* what he's saying because he states that I'm trying "to recast the Canadian tradition." But if the best work *isn't* international in style, in what style is it? If modern Canadian writing isn't international in style, it must be, by definition, markedly unlike any other writing in English. Is this the case? In what kind of style does that most Canadian of writers, Alice Munro, write?

And turning to the more distant past, what Canadian tradition in prose *exists* prior to 1962? What are this tradition's distinguishing marks? Has it invented new forms peculiar to Canada? Did it use language in new and distinctive ways? What are some of its monuments? What are its inter-connections? Whom did it influence? What is the line of descent?

Professor Solecki writes:

... Metcalf's revisionist recasting of the idea of a national literary tradition, with the short story as its focus, makes room for writers like himself who weren't nurtured on *Wacousta* and back issues of *The Canadian Forum*.

Does Professor Solecki *really* imagine that a young Canadian writer getting ready to write twenty-five years ago in 1962 looked to Hugh Garner or Morley Callaghan or harked back to the earlier volumes of Mazo de la Roche?

No young Canadian writer was ever nurtured on *Wacousta* and *The Canadian Forum* and that is the central weakness in Professor Solecki's objections to my assertions. I realize that Professor Solecki is being humorous here and I can quite understand why he feels the uneasy need to be. He humorously cites *Wacousta* and *The Canadian Forum* to stand for "the Canadian tradition" because there are so few titles he could cite with any seriousness and Professor Solecki – even if somewhat confused – is an honest man.

The point is that a young Canadian writer in 1962 was likely never to have *heard* of *Wacousta* but *was* likely to have been in vital contact with, say, Joyce, Beckett, Faulkner, Hemingway, Eliot, Pound, Sartre, Céline, Camus, Kerouac, etc. Fill in your own blanks. Only a writer doomed before beginning *wouldn't* have read these – and more – and digested them.

There was no Canadian tradition available to a young writer of prose. There were no great texts; but, more to the immediate point, *there were in 1962 few available books.* I suspect that what we now think of, vaguely, as 'the Canadian tradition' is largely the McClelland and Stewart New Canadian Library series which was started in 1957 – the brain child, and selections, of one man. This collection of texts cannot be called 'a tradition', cannot be called 'a literature'. Now that Malcolm Ross has retired, a part of the great work is being carried forward by John Moss of the University of Ottawa who with a band of helpers is busy designating this or that volume a Canadian 'Classic'. I cannot feel that this has much to do with a *tradition*. It is rather like a motel owner digging an ancient wishing well and instituting folk customs.

There was no tradition available to a young Canadian writer in 1962 and I very much doubt if there ever will be – at least in the sense in which Professor Solecki seems to be using the word 'tradition'. Writing in English is not contained by national boundaries – Ezra Pound, for example, crossed many frontiers. Canadians do not live in a culture which is hermetically sealed off from outside influence. Young writers are a part of international movements – inescapably. It isn't *possible* for a young Canadian writer to receive 'the Canadian tradition' in pure and unsullied form and it certainly wouldn't be desirable if he or she could. Culture has been international for untold centuries. The only kind of society which still has the *kind* of tradition that Professor Solecki seems to be implying is tribal society.

Professor Solecki knows all this as well as I do. I suspect that

with his uneasy defence of "the Canadian tradition" we are deal-
ing yet again with cultural longing rather than with cultural reality. But part of our difficulties here may result from a far too
casual use of the word 'tradition'.

Four

WHAT DO CRITICS really *mean* when they talk of 'the Canadian tradition'? It's clear that each one means something comically different but what is in their minds when they think of '*a tradition*'? In "What Was Canadian Literature? Taking Stock of the CanLit Industry," an essay first published in *Essays on Canadian Writing* in 1985 – and subsequently adapted for his book *Between Europe and America: The Canadian Tradition in Fiction* (1988) – the critic T.D. MacLulich describes what he considers "the central tradition in our fiction":

... Canadian literature, especially Canadian fiction, has never been notable for its innovations of form. Indeed, its conservatism has contributed to its distinctiveness from American literature. Until very recently, much of the best Canadian fiction has sought to occupy a middle ground, using the conventions of the bourgeois novel to make significant statements about life in particular parts of our country, at particular times. As a result, the central tradition in our fiction is found in the work of writers such as Grove, Callaghan, MacLennan, Buckler, Ross, Mitchell, Wilson, Laurence, Richler, Davies, and Munro. These authors do not produce "popular" literature in the vulgarly commercial sense; yet neither do they rely on superficial treatments of trendy subjects nor on clever tricks played with narrative point of view. They write books that are accessible to a wide readership, and they do so without sacrificing their private vision to commercial demands. We should be encouraging such writing (and some of us are) rather than calling for experimental or language-centred fiction. After all, what will we get if Canadian fiction joins our poetry in adopting the international style? At best, another incarnation of *The*

Studhorse Man. At worst, and a more likely result, more works like Bowering's *A Short Sad Book* and *Burning Water.* The games these works play with Canadian themes do not announce the health of a national tradition, but seem to predict its death, crushed by the weight of excessive self-consciousness.

There is much of interest here:

1) We can recognize the repetition of old arguments. Nationalism versus internationalism with internationalism here presented not as smarmy cosmopolitan sophistication but as vapid, sterile post-modernism.

2) The "conservatism" of Canadian writing is singled out as the tradition's main characteristic. Its lack of formal invention is what mainly distinguishes it from American writing. What many might consider a crippling defect is here elevated to sterling virtue; it's a literary equivalent of a bumper sticker reading 'Canada: Love It or Leave It'.

3) Canadian novels in "the central tradition" are those which use "the conventions of the bourgeois novel to make significant statements about life in particular parts of our country, at particular times." In other words, novels in the tradition of realism.

4) "... the central tradition in our fiction is found in the work of writers such as Grove, Callaghan, MacLennan, Buckler, Ross, Mitchell, Wilson, Laurence, Richler, Davies, and Munro."

5) An "international style" is falsely equated with the postmodern products of Kroetsch and Bowering. What Frye meant in 1967 by "the international style" was writing which had digested the general lessons of modernism.

6) MacLulich mistrusts all "clever tricks." He exhibits a very Canadian mistrust of style and elegance. Lumpishness seems with MacLulich a virtue.

7) The implication is that the future of "the central tradition" will continue to be marked by realism, old-fashionedness result-

ing from cultural insularity, and a down-to-earth lack of "clever tricks."

But let us look now more closely at the writers in MacLulich's central tradition. In what way, exactly, do these writers form a tradition? Did they influence each other? Is their work in any way alike? *Are* they, as MacLulich says they are, all using the conventions of the bourgeois novel? Do they form schools or movements? Do these write in reaction to those?

How *could* anyone yoke together such a disparate crew? Sinclair Ross and Margaret Laurence share a kind of transitional status in terms of their writing, but Alice Munro and Richler write in the international style which MacLulich professes to despise. Alice Munro's writing bulges with "clever tricks" and could scarcely be called realist. What is the relationship between her work and the didactic *exempla* of Callaghan? What connects Richler and Grove other than that Richler called Grove "a good speller"? If Richler belongs to any tradition at all it is to a tradition of North American Jewish writing, writing which is firmly set in the decay of North American Yiddish culture. Richler doubtless feels closer to the work of Joseph Heller and Philip Roth than he does to the work of W.O. Mitchell or Hugh MacLennan. He would also doubtless feel amazed to hear his work described as in "the conventions of the bourgeois novel."

And what about those two old prairie war-horses Grove and Ross? The father and son, as it were, of prairie fiction. In Lorraine McMullen's study of Ross in the Twayne series we read that Ross has read and admires Faulkner, Hemingway, and James Joyce. And then we read: "He has not read Frederick Philip Grove."

What sort of a tradition *is* this?

And what is Robertson Davies – a *realist* writer? – doing in this rather unexamined list? If Michael Ondaatje has to be excluded from the mainstream because of his exoticism, why shouldn't Davies be excluded on precisely the same grounds? If Ondaatje has the exoticism of an orchid, then Davies has the exoticism of a coelacanth – the fish that is described as 'a living fossil'. Davies is unique. Who else in the world is spinning out baroque fables mating Jungian theory with the relentless verbosity of Thomas Love Peacock?

And how does Ethel Wilson – the most under-valued writer Canada has produced – fit into this "central tradition"? Alice Munro admires Ethel Wilson's writing, but how does Ethel Wilson's exquisite style relate to that of Buckler the Purple Boomer? What yokes her delicacy to the clodhoppery of Grove or the flat, second-hand Britishness of MacLennan?

And how do these writers see *themselves*? Do they see *themselves* as forming "the central tradition"? Callaghan has said over and over again that he considers himself a North American writer; he claims Hemingway as a central influence. Richler *fled* Canada. Alice Munro learned her craft at the feet of Sherwood Anderson and Eudora Welty. Margaret Laurence once said, "I think the thing that matters least about a novel is whether it's Canadian or American or English or African...."

If these writers constitute a "central tradition," then I must confess that I don't know what a tradition *is*. But I suggest that they constitute nothing of the kind; their work is a more or less random conglomeration of individual books. They're on the lists of this or that critic as being 'the tradition' simply because they somehow survived Canada's indifference to them. (*How* they survived is a question to which I'll return.) In brief, then, these books are our 'tradition' of prose fiction because they're more or less the only books there are; these rough-hewn monoliths are all that stand above the flat desolation of the first sixty years of the century. There are so sadly few of them.

But mere survival does not constitute a 'tradition'. A tradition is alive, various, densely populated, intricate. It is interconnected. It is like a river which accommodates within its general flow differing currents and eddies and whirlpools and backwaters. A tradition teaches and trains. It is like a family which is constantly expanding yet managing somehow to contain and sustain contradictory personalities and disparate aims and ambitions.

The older writers on MacLulich's list in no sense belonged to that sort of tradition. That sort of tradition did not exist in Canada. Their books were isolated events and they themselves tended to live in literary isolation. Buckler was a recluse. Ross left Canada on his retirement to live in Europe. Callaghan has remained largely aloof from literary life. Caught in the conservative Canadian time-warp, MacLennan continued teaching at McGill and plodding away on novels which were old-fashioned while he was writing them; it was Smith, Dudek, Layton, and John Sutherland who variously launched themselves into the ferment of the international literary currents.

In his introduction to *Other Canadians* in 1947 John Sutherland wrote of A.J.M. Smith:

... Mr. Smith knows it is utter nonsense to talk about a "tradition" of Canadian poetry. We could only use the word tradition if we believed that the poetry was so blended with the life of the country that it was able to reach into the present and influence its course.

Sutherland makes an essential point here: *a tradition reaches into the present and influences its course.*

Every day of my life is lived with other writers. Their shapes and forms, a use of language peculiar to them, this one's tone, that loved one's flash and filigree – all this informs my work. My writing draws on the account that belongs to all of us. My converse is with Whitman, Hopkins, Tennyson, Crowe Ransom, Larkin, Layton, Newlove, Heaney – the living *and* the dead.

Do older writers on MacLulich's list reach into *our* present? Can our younger writers draw on them? Can we *seriously* postulate a Canadian tradition in fiction founded on *Wacousta, The Master of the Mill, Two Solitudes,* and *Jake and the Kid*? I would suggest that those writers who most vibrantly live on for us are writers whose work was demanding at the time it was written. Our 'Classics' – duly stamped with John Moss's *imprimatur* – simply aren't classic *enough*; they're simple books, often technically inept, quickly exhausted. Put briefly, we don't have a Canadian tradition in fiction before about 1962 because hardly anything from those earlier years reaches out to touch and engage us.

John Sutherland raises another essential point: "We could only use the word tradition if we believed that the poetry *was ... blended with the life of the country ...*" (emphasis added).

A literature is a relationship between books and readers. A tradition implies an audience. A tradition honours and bequeaths; it is a gift handed down from generation to generation. A literature is a living thing; it is the involvement of writers and readers, of publishers, printers, scholars, critics, reviewers, teachers, librarians, booksellers, book-collectors, antiquarians, bibliographers, and historians, in the cherishing of language.

Without an audience a literature cannot exist.

I said earlier that I would return to the question of *how* certain of the books by writers on MacLulich's list had managed to survive Canada's indifference. Let us consider the case of Sinclair Ross's *As for Me and My House*. The book was published by Reynal and Hitchcock in New York in 1941. Lorraine McMullen in her Twayne study of Ross writes:

> A few copies of the novel were imported for the Canadian market by McClelland and Stewart, but in all, only a few hundred copies were sold. Not until publication of the paperback edition in 1957 did the novel achieve the recognition it deserved.

Recognition from whom? The New Canadian Library series in which the book appeared in 1957 is not designed to appeal to and does not reach a wide or popular audience. I think it would be fair to say that this Canadian 'Classic' has been read mainly by teachers and students. And who now reads *The Well* and *Whir of Gold*? In 1974 *Sawbones Memorial* was published by McClelland and Stewart and in 1978 it was reissued in the New Canadian Library.

Subsequently Ross wrote another novel which McClelland and Stewart rejected; it remains unpublished.

Ernest Buckler fits into much the same sort of pattern. *The Mountain and the Valley* was published in the USA and Canada in 1952 and published as a New Canadian Library paperback in 1961. Again, the audience is made up almost exclusively of teachers and students. Who now reads Buckler's other works? Who now reads *The Cruelest Month, Ox Bells and Fireflies,* and *Whirligig*?

There is something disturbing about two of the chief pillars of 'the Canadian tradition' being essentially one-book men. There is something disturbing in the inadequacy of most of their other now-unread writing. Disturbing also is the history of critical response to *As for Me and My House* and *The Mountain and the Valley*; that response suggests that the critics have decided on canonization whatever literary difficulties and purple defects they are forced to ignore or stumble over.

Never one to fear rushing in, John Moss wrote in *Patterns of Isolation in English Canadian Fiction* (1974): "Time and again *As for Me and My House* has been called a minor Canadian classic. Surely it is time, and we have achieved sufficient maturity and good taste, for the delimiting adjectives to be dropped."

Well...*no*.

(Essential essays by Morton L. Ross and Lawrence Mathews on the critical response to both books can be found in *The Bumper Book*, ed. J. Metcalf.)

It would be tedious to go on. Suffice it to say that in nearly every case we can equate 'the Canadian tradition' with the New Canadian Library series. These books do not connect with any ordinary book-buying public; they are not in a relationship with a readership. The reputations of these books were created and are fostered by academics to serve dubious academic and nationalist ends.

In the next section I'd like to draw together some of the threads we've been talking about so far – the idea of a tradition, the lack of an audience, nationalism, the virtual invention of our literature by academics – by examining the way that cultural nationalists and academics have responded to one particular Canadian book: *In the Village of Viger* by Duncan Campbell Scott. I want what I have to say about this book to sum up much of my argument here and to suggest and stand for much that I haven't actually spelled out.

Five

In the Village of Viger by Duncan Campbell Scott was first published in 1896 by Copeland and Day in Boston. This first edition is extremely scarce if not rare. I know two dealers in Canadian first editions who currently have recently-acquired copies of the book – Nicky Drumbolis in Toronto and William Hoffer in Vancouver – but both say that the copies are the first they have come across in two decades of bookselling.

Copeland and Day was a firm dedicated to aesthetic rather than commercial concerns. Their interest was in producing precious books beautifully. They had connections with the William Morris-influenced fine press movement in England and their first productions were editions of such *Yellow Book* writers as Lionel Johnson, John Davidson, and Oscar Wilde bound up from imported British sheets. They also co-published with such rarefied British small presses as Elkin Mathews. Their mission was to marry small press standards of book design with commercial practice. Day was extremely wealthy and, for a while at least, money was no object. The press began publishing in 1893 and was dissolved six years later in 1899.

With such standards and with such writers, it was inevitable that the audience was circumscribed and the print runs small. Nicky Drumbolis of Letters bookstore offers as an educated guess that Copeland and Day printed 750 copies of *In the Village of Viger*. His reason for believing this is that the company printed 500 copies of Archibald Lampman's *Lyrics of Earth* and 500 copies of Francis Sherman's *Matins* in the same year as Scott's book. But whatever, the outside figure for *In the Village of Viger* would have been 1000 copies.

When Copeland and Day was dissolved in 1899, an accounting was made of stock. The following figures are derived from Joe W. Kraus's *Messrs. Copeland & Day*:

In the Village of Viger. By Duncan Campbell Scott.
Issued in March 1896 in an edition of an unknown size but most probably between 750 and 1000 copies. In May 1899, 578 copies remained unsold.

Lyrics of Earth. By Archibald Lampman.
a) Trade issue: 500 copies printed in March 1896 of which 36 bound copies and 194 sets of sheets remained unsold in May 1899.
b) Handmade paper issue: 50 copies of which 42 remained unsold.

Matins. By Francis Sherman.
a) Trade issue: 500 copies printed in November 1896 of which 106 copies remained unsold in May 1899.
b) Handmade paper issue: 35 copies. Number that remained unsold is unknown.

Labor and the Angel. By Duncan Campbell Scott.
Printed in October 1898 in an edition of an unknown size but most probably 500. In May 1899, 384 copies remained unsold.

If the print run of *In the Village of Viger* was 1000, this means that 422 copies were sold; if the print run was 750, this means that 172 copies were sold. We do not know what happened to the remaining stock. It was obviously not in wild demand. It may have sold slowly. It may have been remaindered. It may have been destroyed. Nicky Drumbolis suggests – citing the example of Lampman's *Lyrics of Earth* – that one explanation for *In the Village of Viger*'s rarity is that possibly not all of the printing was bound up.

How many copies of the book made their way into Canada? It is impossible to know but we should suspect that very few copies indeed crossed the border. Although the book was by a Canadian, the audience for the book would undoubtedly have been American. Copeland and Day was publishing more or less for a coterie, a small élite of Americans with aesthetic urges who probably bought the books as much for their bindings, typography, and illustrations as for their content; it is difficult to imagine much of a literary audience in Canada for Scott at that time and even more difficult to imagine Canadian aesthetes in any number.

Nelson Ball, in Paris, Ontario, another of the best-known dealers in Canadian first editions, says that he has never had a copy of *In the Village of Viger* and adds that copies of *Lyrics of Earth* and *Matins* he has handled have all come from dealers in the United States and never from Canada. He says he would describe Scott's book as 'rare'.

In the Village of Viger is not in Bernard Amtmann's *Contributions to a Short-Title Catalogue of Canadiana* – a listing of all the books that he catalogued – and neither is it listed as having come up for sale in Canadian book auctions from 1967 to 1982.

Pat McGahern of J. Patrick McGahern Books Inc. of Ottawa, one of Canada's most respected and scholarly dealers in antiquarian books, has never had a copy of *In the Village of Viger* in twenty years of bookselling. This is highly significant because Ottawa was Scott's hometown and McGahern has, over the years, handled everything else of Scott's even down to such ephemera as his privately printed Christmas cards. McGahern's experience of the trade has convinced him that far fewer than 50 copies of the 1896 edition of Scott's book circulated in Canada.

In the Village of Viger was first published in Canada in 1945. Scott had attempted to get the book printed in 1926 by McClelland and Stewart but they declined. The 1945 edition was published by The Ryerson Press in a dull brown utilitarian binding and dust jacket though the text was enhanced with charming drawings by Thoreau MacDonald. In the 1940s, a typical Ryerson Press print run was between 500 and 750 copies. It is probable that 750 copies of *In the Village of Viger* were published. Copies of the 1945 edition in mint condition and with dust jackets in mint condition have been until recently quite easy to find. The reason for this is that when The Ryerson Press was purchased by

McGraw-Hill in 1970 a vast sale of unsold Ryerson stock was held in a hockey arena (an essentially Canadian story, this, and possibly symbolic of something or other) and previously unopened cases of *In the Village of Viger* were remaindered.

If we add these facts and likelihoods and hints together and err heavily on the side of generosity, we could say that perhaps 50 copies of the 1896 edition entered Canada and that between 1945 and 1970 The Ryerson Press sold 350 copies of the reprint. This gives us a total sales figure in Canada of 400 copies in seventy-four years.

In 1928 Raymond Knister dedicated his anthology *Canadian Short Stories* to Duncan Campbell Scott and wrote in his introduction:

> And a perfect flowering of art is embodied in one volume, *In the Village of Viger*, by Duncan Campbell Scott. It is work which has had an unobtrusive influence; but it stands out after thirty years as the most satisfyingly individual contribution to the Canadian short story.

In 1945 the critic B.K. Sandwell said, in review of the reprint, that it "has long been cherished by friends of the poet and deserves wide circulation."

Sandwell's comment suggests *how* unobtrusive *In the Village of Viger* actually was. Knister's "unobtrusive influence" is balanced by his following "but." He is saying in the nicest possible way that Scott's book is unknown to all but such as he; his "unobtrusive influence" is an exhibition of exquisite politeness, a gloss on an unfortunate truth, a younger writer's tactful tribute to a respected older writer.

The book was reprinted for the second time in the New Canadian Library series in 1973.

WHAT SORT of book is it?

It is a collection of ten stories all of which are set in the village of Viger and all of which concern the doings of the village's inhabitants. W.H. New writes in *Dreams of Speech and Violence: The Art of the Short Story in Canada and New Zealand*:

> Like many other nineteenth-century story collections, *In the Village of Viger* assembles a variety of conventional patterns into a kind of miscellany. There is a sentimental fable in 'The Bobolink', a comic anecdote in 'The Wooing of Monsieur Cuerrier', a romantic tale in 'The Tragedy of the Seigniory', a folk-tale in 'The Pedler', a melodrama in 'The Desjardins', a sketch in 'Josephine Labrosse', and elements of allegory in 'Sedan'.

The collection is prefaced by the following poem:

Whoever has from toil and stress
Put into ports of idleness,
And watched the gleaming thistledown
Wheel in the soft air lazily blown;
Or leaning on the shady rail,
Beneath the poplars, silver pale,
Eyed in the shallow amber pools
The black perch voyaging in schools;
Or heard the fisherman outpour
His strange and questionable lore,
While the cream-blossomed basswood-trees
Boomed like an organ with the bees;
Or by blind fancy held aloof
Has startled with prosaic hoof
Beneath the willows in the shade,
The wooing of a pretty maid;
And traced the sharp or genial air
Of human nature everywhere:
Might find perchance the wandered fire,
Around St. Joseph's sparkling spire;
And wearied with the fume and strife,
The complex joys and ills of life,

Might for an hour his worry staunch,
In pleasant Viger by the Blanche.

Doggerel though this may be – and in places near-incomprehensible doggerel – it is clear enough that Scott's intention is to offer the reader in "pleasant Viger by the Blanche" an idyll of French-Canadian life.

I want to suggest something of the style and flavour of the writing by two quotations. The first is the opening paragraph of the story "Sedan":

One of the pleasantest streets in Viger was that which led from the thoroughfare of the village to the common. It was a little street with little houses, but it looked as if only happy people lived there. The enormous old willows which shaded it through its whole length made a perpetual shimmer of shadow and sun, and towered so above the low cottages that they seemed to have crept under the guardian trees to rest and doze a while. There was something idyllic about this contented spot; it seemed to be removed from the rest of the village, to be on the boundaries of Arcadia, the first inlet to its pleasant, dreamy fields. In the spring the boys made a veritable Arcadia of it, coming there in bands, cutting the willows for whistles, and entering into a blithe contest for supremacy in making them, accompanying their labours by a perpetual sounding of their pleasant pipes, as if a colony of uncommon birds had taken up their homes in the trees. Even in the winter there was something pleasant about it; the immense boles of the willows, presiding over the collection of houses, seemed to protect them, and the sunshine had always a suggestion of warmth as it dwelt in the long branches. It was on this street, just a little distance from the corner, that Paul Arbique kept his inn, which was famous in its way. He called it The Turenne, after the renowned commander of that name, for they had the same birthplace, and

Arbique himself had been a soldier, as his medals would testify. The location was favourable for such a house as Arbique was prepared to keep, and in choosing it he appealed to a crotchet in man which makes it pleasanter for him to go around the corner for anything he may require. A pleasant place it was, particularly in summer. The very exterior had an air about it, the green blinds and the green slatted door, and the shadows from the willow-leaves playing over the legend "Fresh Buttermilk," a sign dear to the lover of simple pleasures.

The second quotation is the opening paragraph of "The Bobolink":

It was the sunniest corner in Viger where old Garnaud had built his cabin – his cabin, for it could not be called a house. It was only of one storey, with a kitchen behind, and a workshop in front, where Etienne Garnaud mended the shoes of Viger. He had lived there by himself ever since he came from St. Valérie; everyone knew his story, everyone liked him. A merry heart had the old shoemaker; it made a merry heart to see him bending his white head with its beautiful features above his homely work, and to hear his voice in a high cadence of good-humoured song. The broad window of his cabin was covered with a shutter hinged at the top, which was propped up by a stick slanted from the window-sill. In the summer the sash was removed, and through the opening came the even sound of the Blanche against the bridge piers, or the scythe-whetting from some hidden meadow. From it there was a view of a little pool of the stream where the perch jumped clear into the sun, and where a birch growing on the bank threw a silver shadow-bridge from side to side. Farther up, too, were the willows that wore the yellow tassels in the spring, and the hollow where burr-marigolds were brown-golden in August. On the hill slope stood a delicate maple that reddened the moment summer had gone, which old Etienne watched with a sigh and a shake of the head.

What to say of writing like this?

It reminds me inescapably of a scene in my novel *Going Down Slow* where Howie Bunceford, the Head of the school's English Department, takes over the innovative young teacher's class to demonstrate to him and to his students what *real* writing is all about:

> Hands loosely clasped, looking like a minister inviting a congregation to prayer, Howie said,
> "... and so I'd like to share with you, then, a beautiful descriptive passage written by the famous British author Sir Compton Mackenzie. Perhaps we can't all write so beautifully ourselves but we *can* all aspire to lofty goals, can't we?"
> He smiled.
> He opened *The Oxford Book of English Prose*.
> "Quite, quite silent now," he said.
> Eyes lifted to the sunlight at the tall window, he waited.
> In unctuous voice he began to read.
> "Some four-and-twenty miles from Curtain Wells on the Great West Road is a tangle of briers among whose blossoms an old damask rose is sometimes visible. If the curious traveller should pause and examine this fragrant wilderness, he will plainly perceive the remains of an ancient garden, and if he be of an imaginative character of mind will readily recall the legend of the Sleeping Beauty in her mouldering palace; for some enchantment still enthralls the spot, so that he who bravely dares the thorns is well rewarded with pensive dreams and, as he lingers a while gathering the flowers or watching their petals flutter to the green shadows beneath, will haply see elusive Beauty hurry past ..."

Mackenzie's writing is too nauseating to quote more.

The style of *In the Village of Viger* is not, in the main, as bad as Mackenzie's but it is drawn from the same models and exhibits the same tired tricks and tropes, the scuffed baggage of a worn-out culture and language.

It was Cyril Connolly in *Enemies of Promise*, I believe, who called attention to the word 'little' as a near-infallible indicator of sentimentality; Scott's "little street with little houses" that "seemed to have crept under the guardian trees to rest and doze a while" is unadulterated saccharine but he also displays the bankruptcy of his language in his ponderous classical allusion, in the self-consciously 'elevated' rhetoric of his sentence inversions, and in his 'poetic' nut-brown-maid vocabulary.

This horribly *wrought* style with its soft focus and imprecise diction distances reality managing to present, for example, a gang of scruffy kids making whistles as being somehow like the idealized youths depicted on Greek vases playing Panpipes; the village boys come to the willow trees "in bands" – the suggestion here is of religious procession – and enter into "a blithe contest" in the making of "their pleasant pipes" turning "this contented spot" into "a veritable Arcadia."

There is not much point, however, in belabouring the writing's obvious defects – "A merry heart had the old shoemaker; it made a merry heart to see him bending his white head with its beautiful features above his homely work, and to hear his voice in a high cadence of good-humoured song" – because *In the Village of Viger* is genre-writing and such sentimentality, artificiality, and conde-scension as Scott exhibits are an expected part of the genre. The idyll is the literary equivalent of a Fabergé 'Easter Egg'; it is a pleasant work descriptive of rural or pastoral life written for the entertainment of sophisticated urban readers and its tradition goes back to the Greeks. We do not turn to the idyll or pastoral for searing exposés of rural incest or non-unionized grape-picking.

The opening paragraphs of the two stories from *In the Village of Viger* that I've quoted give a slightly unfair impression of the book as a whole; not all of the writing is that cloying. When he is not working the lyric vein and loading every rift with ore, Scott can write briskly and precisely as he does in the openings of such stories as "Paul Farlotte" and "The Tragedy of the Seigniory." His dialogue tends to be a trifle stilted and 'stagey' but that is mainly because his characters are puppets who speak in forms and tones appropriate to their melodramas. When he relaxes – in the gentle comedy of "The Wooing of Monsieur Cuerrier" and in the village gossip of "The Little Milliner" – the dialogue improves vastly and suggests that this could have become Scott's central strength.

Attempts have been made by some recent critics to suggest that *In the Village of Viger* is something other than what it appears to be; it is marked, they say, by a certain realism revolutionary for its time. It has been pointed out that the village is not an idealized paradise, that the book is not, in fact, an idyll at all because some of the stories involve drunkenness, cynical manipulation of emotions, insanity, and murder. Such, admittedly, is not the stuff of the *Eclogues* or of *Daphnis and Chloe,* but these 'realities' do not rend the dreamy fabric of "pleasant Viger" because they are not presented in any *immediate* way. We remain outside these people. They are characters in tales, 'folk', quaint peasants who live quaint *habitant* lives. Reality is muffled and hollowed by the flabbiness and decorum of the language and by the manner of the tales' telling.

"The Tragedy of the Seigniory" is not a tragedy but a melodrama; the murder of Hugo Armand Theophile Rioux by Louis Bois is a polite affair, an accident, the mechanical result of a series of coincidences:

> He tried to utter a cry, but sank into his chair stricken dumb; for death had not yet softened the lines of desperate cunning on the face, which, in spite of the scars of a wild life, he recognized as that of Hugo Armand Theophile Rioux.

This is the language of the silent movies.

"The Tragedy of the Seigniory" is not intended to be realistic; all it has to commend it is the twists and turns of its plot; it is not concerned with the personalities of slayer or slain; it is not concerned with evil. Nothing about this story will haunt us as we are haunted by, say, Bill Sykes' murder of Nancy. Similarly, Paul Arbique in the story "Sedan" may be a drunkard but it is a sedate and *literary* drunkenness, a device of plot.

In an essay entitled "Local Colour in Canadian Fiction," first published in the *University of Toronto Quarterly* in 1959 and later anthologized in *Twentieth Century Essays on Confederation Literature*, William H. Magee writes:

> The basic challenge to all these storytellers, the difficulty of finding a fictional frame of plot and characterization appropriate to lauding local atmosphere, baffled Scott more than it did many a mediocre writer. Instead of domestic or humorous plots, or even the non-artistic conflicts of didactic local colourists, he fell into using mystery stories and a plot suspense incompatible with the local charm. In various stories involving such characters as a robber, a madman, a murderer, and a mysterious pedler, Scott draws on a purely fictional tradition of life for a frame for the manners.

This is inelegantly expressed but to the point. *In the Village of Viger* remains, whatever recent critics may say, a miscellany of *habitant* stories; it is a minor book by a minor writer, a book of purely historical interest. If one has a taste for such period-pieces, it might be described, I suppose, as 'charming'.

The importance and interest of the book lie in what the critics have done to it and why.

SCOTT'S REPUTATION was slow to develop. In the essay on him in *Canadian Writers and Their Works* (Poetry Series, Volume Two) Gordon Johnston writes:

> During his lifetime, Scott did not receive a great deal of critical attention. It is possible (and quite common) to exaggerate this neglect; nevertheless, perhaps because of the

state of Canadian criticism and culture until about 1950, Scott was difficult to "see."

One of the first critical assessments of *In the Village of Viger* appeared in 1924 in *Highways of Canadian Literature* by J.D. Logan and Donald G. French:

> *In the Village of Viger* (1896) by Duncan Campbell Scott is a little volume of prose tales of French Canada, published in Boston by Copeland and Day. These stories affect the heart and imagination with a reality and sense of actuality as if one had dwelt in Viger and had daily come face to face with ... [here follows a list of the names of several characters in the stories].
>
> The reality and veracity of Dr. Scott's character delineation produces exquisite and infallible character-vignettes, or Rembrandtesque word-etchings, lovely in 'values' and in spiritual *chiaroscuro* – depths within depths of a single character as in Charles Desjardins in the tragic story of *The Desjardins*. Yet in his handling of the tragic he awakens, not a pity that produces fear or horror or disgust, but a gentle pity that engenders sympathy. We appreciate the 'little milliner's' loyalty – begotten of pure love – to her rascal lover, a common thief. The skilful sympathetic handling of the subject gives to love a new dignity and to loyalty a new grandeur. The pathos moves to a rise and fall, but never so overwhelms the emotions as to cause tears; rather does it subdue the soul and leave in the heart of the reader a gentle welling up of sympathy, a benignant sense of fellowship with finite and erring humanity, and a tender peace. When a reader finishes one of Dr. Scott's stories of the pathetic episode – *The Little Milliner, The Desjardins, Sedan, Paul Farlotte* – he experiences no violent wrench of the heart-strings – sheds no tears – but is gently and sweetly touched; feels with the unfortunate and afflicted; sees the veil that obscures the hard workaday world lifted; and beholds life and the world

suffused with a 'grey-eyed loveliness'. This is all superb artistry in emotional and spiritual love, by one who has had intimate glimpses into the human heart and into the stern face of sublimity in human character and in life.

As oleaginous a pat of prose as I've read in a long time.

(Note that in 1924 Logan felt it necessary to explain that the book had been published in Boston by Copeland and Day.)

It was also in 1924 that Archibald MacMechan published *Headwaters of Canadian Literature*; he mentions Scott neither as poet nor as fiction writer.

Desmond Pacey in the introduction to *A Book of Canadian Stories* (1947) writes:

> His subject-matter is as romantic as that of his contemporaries, but to its handling he brings a delicacy and subtlety of touch which seriously alters its effect. To set his chief volume of short stories, *In the Village of Viger*, beside Parker's *Pierre and His People*, is to be struck by many sharp contrasts. Where Parker's work is flamboyant and highly coloured, Scott's is quiet, self-effacing, and subdued. Overstatement has been replaced by understatement, crude melodrama by refined suggestion and symbolism, Parker's prodigality of words by a deliberate economy of utterance. One feels in Scott's work that every word has been first weighed and considered and finally chosen with a full realization of all its connotations. All parts of the stories have been similarly deliberated upon: characters, setting, and events are blended and shaped into a satisfying artistic whole.

Gordon Roper, Rupert Schieder, and S. Ross Beharriell in the *Literary History of Canada* (1965) discuss *In the Village of Viger* as one among many collections of tales about French-Canadian life:

> Most of these writers were visitors to the *habitant* scenes they told about. Their tone is bucolic, as if they are remem-

bering with some quiet pleasure the village scene and the people with whom they had spent some pleasant hours while on a vacation. The sentiment is marked, but not usually heavy; the humour and pathos equally light.

They observe:

> Duncan Campbell Scott published one of the most skilful collections in his *In the Village of Viger*....

The entry on Scott in *The Oxford Companion to Canadian History and Literature* compiled in 1967 by Norah Story refers to

> ... Scott's two collections of deceptively simple short stories that are still read with pleasure: *In the Village of Viger* (Boston, 1896) and *The Witching of Elspie* (1923). The earlier volume is light in touch, though it varies from the humorous 'The Wooing of Monsieur Cuerrier' to the eerie 'The Pedler'.

In the entry "Fiction in English: Short Stories" we read:

> The descriptive powers and some of the artistry of Duncan Campbell Scott's poetry can be found in his stories of *habitant* life in Quebec: *In the Village of Viger* (London [sic], 1896) in which its humorous side is portrayed, and *The Witching of Elspie* (1923) which deals with its darker aspects and superstitions.

In the context of remarks about W.H. Drummond and English-Canadian condescension to French Canadians, Elizabeth Waterston writes in *Survey: A Short History of Canadian Literature* (1973): "Duncan Campbell Scott also exploited the comic value of the superstitious villagers in *In the Village of Viger*, 1896, and other stories."

In *The Canadian Century* (1973), A.J.M. Smith describes the book as: "delicate and sensitive local colour sketches of life in rural Quebec."

Let us recapitulate.

Up until 1973 there seems to be almost general agreement about two things: first, Scott is writing "local colour sketches"; second, his writing is far superior to the work of others in the same genre. Personally, I consider Scott's fiction shallow and decorative; he writes badly in an exhausted tradition. All those previous judgements praising his artistry must have been comparative; I confess that I haven't had the stomach for *Pierre and His People*, but I would maintain that if Gilbert Parker and a dozen others are grandly awful *that* does not make Scott accomplished.

Logan's opinion about *anything* is obviously irrelevant; I quoted him at such length simply because one rarely comes across prose of such *orgasmic* unctuousness. Pacey praises Scott's artistry and describes the stories as "romantic." Roper, Schieder, and Beharriell seem to have considered the stories as "light" in their emotional impact. Norah Story calls them "light in touch" and says that the book portrays the "humorous side" of *habitant* life. Elizabeth Waterston says the book "exploited the comic value of the superstitious villagers." A.J.M. Smith describes the stories as "delicate and sensitive local colour sketches of life in rural Quebec."

We might note that not one of these critics seems to feel that the drunkenness in "Sedan" or the insanity in "The Desjardins" or the murder in "The Tragedy of the Seigniory" mars the general 'lightness' of the volume. I have suggested that the reason for this is that Scott's readers simply don't take these matters as in any way *real*; the accidental murder of the young master by the devoted servant is a purely artificial and *literary* event.

IN 1973, *In the Village of Viger* – along with a selection of Scott's later stories – was reissued as a paperback in the New Canadian Library series with an introduction by Professor Stan Dragland.

Professor Dragland's view of the book was revisionist and was seized on subsequently by other academics and by cultural nationalists and inflated alarmingly.

It is necessary to quote Professor Dragland at some length:

> ... we soon find that Viger is in danger of being swallowed by the metropolis of which it is one of the "outlying wards." In one direction, Maurice Ruelle's window commands "miles of broken country"; in the other, the sky is "luminous with the reflection of a thousand gas-lamps." So Viger is a village in transition: "New houses had already commenced to spring up in all directions, and there was a large influx of the labouring population which overflows from large cities." This sentence comes from the opening paragraphs of "The Little Milliner" which not only set the scene for that story but introduce an urban undercurrent which surfaces several times in the volume. It affects the Little Milliner through the crime her relative commits in the city; it is where Josephine Labrosse's mother goes to find work; it provides furniture buyers and prospective husbands for Eloise Ruelle in "No. 68 Rue Alfred de Musset." And it may be no accident that a fixation with the assembly-line mechanism we associate with cities is the downfall of Guy St. Denis in "Paul Farlotte."

The motif of the city, then, appears in several of the stories. And there are other details which work for Scott both within particular stories, and as a rhythm of structural links between the stories. One connecting thread is the image of a bird, caged or free, most central in "The Bobolink," but variously significant in "The Wooing of Monsieur Cuerrier," "Josephine Labrosse," "The Pedler," and "Paul Farlotte." Striking a more sombre note in "The Little Milliner" is "Daigneau's pit" with its "green slime" that makes the flesh creep, and in "The Desjardins" the "marshy field" where "you could thrust down a long pole and not touch bottom." Swamp and city motifs are part of the ironic underside of pastoral Viger, and would tip the reader off to the presence in Viger of something more than the pleasant relief from our cares that Scott promises in his opening poem, even if there were no other irony in the book.

In fact, some of the settings are ironic, like the situation of the Arbique Inn in "Sedan": "There was something idyllic about this contented spot; it seemed to be removed from the rest of the village, to be on the boundaries of Arcadia, the first inlet to its pleasant, dreamy field." [The text has "fields."] The key word is "seemed," because Arcadia is not known for misers, alcoholics, or persecuted orphans and Germans, all of which we find in the story. "The Bobolink," too, about the initiation into disillusionment of old Etienne and his young friend, the blind girl, is ironically set in "the sunniest corner of Viger." The story is the more effective because we are allowed to detect the irony in the setting for ourselves, and because Scott leaves it to us to figure out why the positive act of freeing a caged bird should create sorrow and loneliness in the lives of the releasers.

In Viger there is as much tragedy as we are likely to encounter in less idyllic surroundings. And not only the tragedy of circumstance we find in "Sedan" or the tragedy of hereditary weakness examined in "The Desjardins" or "Paul Farlotte." There is also the tragedy caused by human nature, which Scott knew could be "sharp" as well as "genial" (the terms are from the opening poem). Eloise Ruelle, in "No. 68 Rue Alfred de Musset," is as unfeeling and alive to the main chance as Becky Thatcher, and therefore quite capable of compounding her brother's personal tragedy on her way to a long, successful career. The story of Eloise Ruelle shows Scott interested in human nature as it is, not as it may be romanticised black or white. He convinces us that his characters are real by subtle use of irony and understatement, both tools of realism.

... By writing honestly about people and places he knew from experience, he helped engineer the revolution to realism in Canadian fiction for which Sara Jeannette Duncan, Frederick Philip Grove, Sinclair Ross, and Ringuet are better known. For historical reasons, then, and because he created a small but important body of work worth reading for itself, he deserves our attention.

Let us summarize the main points Professor Dragland makes:

1) Viger is a village in transition; in the near future it will be swallowed up by the expanding city. The influence of the city on the village constitutes "an urban undercurrent which surfaces several times" introducing negative or destructive elements into the rural idyll. Professor Dragland calls this "The motif of the city."

2) There is also a swamp motif. "Swamp and city motifs are part of the ironic underside of pastoral Viger, and would tip the reader off to the presence in Viger of something more than the pleasant relief from our cares that Scott promises in his opening poem...."

3) Scott "convinces us that his characters are real by subtle use of irony and understatement, both tools of realism."

4) Because Scott wrote "honestly about people and places he knew from experience, he helped engineer the revolution to realism in Canadian fiction...."

If Professor Dragland can persuade us that there is an "ironic underside of pastoral Viger" and that "Swamp and city motifs are part of the ironic underside," he can then claim Scott on the strength of that irony, irony being one of the "tools of realism," as a realist and one of the founders of modern writing in Canada.

Let us examine Professor Dragland's claims.

The word 'motif' as used in reference to literature means a particular idea or dominant feeling – often embodied in a physical detail or class of details – which recurs throughout the work helping to form or intensify the work's main theme.

Professor Dragland claims that *In the Village of Viger* deploys a 'swamp motif' which is a part of the book's "ironic underside." Professor Dragland doesn't actually tell us what the 'swamp motif' means but I assume that we are intended to think of the swamp as being in some way non-idyllic and possibly bubbling away with symbolic evil – rather like an early Hammer film – and therefore demonstrative of irony on Scott's part.

There are, in fact, only *two* references in all ten stories to anything remotely resembling a swamp and *neither* reference is negative.

The first reference comes in the opening paragraph of "The Little Milliner" but it is a reference not to a swamp but to a flooded mine shaft. The context of the reference is important; Scott refers to "Daigneau's pit" in a list of desirable things that will be no more when the suburbs overtake the village. It would seem that Professor Dragland has either misunderstood the passage or distorted it in his revisionist zeal. It is crystal clear that Scott is not implying an evil 'underside' in his unusually evocative description of Daigneau's pit with its delightfully scary slime but is, rather, mourning the impending loss of the pit and the consequent loss of texture and richness in the children's lives.

Here is the passage:

> But when the time came for Viger to be mentioned in the city papers as one of the outlying wards, what a change there would be! There would be no unfenced fields, full of little inequalities and covered with short grass; there would be no deep pools, where the quarries had been, and where the boys pelted the frogs; there would be no more beech-groves, where the children could gather nuts; and the dread pool, which had filled the shaft where old Daigneau, years ago, mined for gold, would cease to exist. But in the meantime, the boys of Viger roamed over the unclosed fields and pelted the frogs, and the boldest ventured to roll huge stones into Daigneau's pit, and only waited to see the green slime come working up to the surface before scampering away, their flesh creeping with the idea that it was old Daig-

neau himself who was stirring up the water in a rage.

The second and only other reference to a 'swamp' comes in the opening paragraph of "The Desjardins":

Just at the foot of the hill, where the bridge crossed the Blanche, stood one of the oldest houses in Viger. It was built of massive timbers. The roof curved and projected beyond the eaves, forming the top of a narrow veranda. The whole house was painted a dazzling white except the window-frames, which were green. There was a low stone fence between the road and the garden, where a few simple flowers grew. Beyond the fence was a row of Lombardy poplars, some of which had commenced to die out. On the opposite side of the road was a marshy field, where by day the marsh marigolds shone, and by night, the fire-flies. There were places in this field where you could thrust down a long pole and not touch bottom. In the fall a few musk-rats built a house there, in remembrance of the time when it was a favourite wintering-ground. In the spring the Blanche came up and flowed over it. Beyond that again the hill curved round, with a scarped, yellowish slope.

Professor Dragland's 'swamp' is, in fact, "a marshy field" and obviously a pleasing one since marigolds shone there by day and fire-flies by night. On fine summer evenings, Philippe and Adèle would walk alongside the field to watch the fire-flies.

There is not much here of "ironic underside."

There *is* no 'swamp motif'.

There are no swamps.

And what of the "urban undercurrent" and "motif of the city"? Professor Dragland says that "Swamp and city motifs are part of the ironic underside of pastoral Viger." Again, he does not spell out what he means. We must assume that he means that Scott is presenting "pastoral Viger" ironically, that Scott is being 'realistic' by revealing in ironic and understated ways that Viger is not as idyllic as it appears to be. All this is irritatingly *vague*. We are left to assume further that the sophistication and corruption of the city are destructive of Viger's idyllic peace but Professor Dragland's instances of the effect of the "urban undercurrent" on the villagers are limp and unpersuasive:

> It affects the Little Milliner through the crime her relative commits in the city; it is where Josephine Labrosse's mother goes to find work; it provides furniture buyers and prospective husbands for Eloise Ruelle in "No. 68 Rue Alfred de Musset." And it may be no accident that a fixation with the assembly-line mechanism we associate with cities is the downfall of Guy St. Denis in "Paul Farlotte."

We might note that the Little Milliner had just come to Viger presumably from the city and wasn't a villager at all, that the city gave Madame Labrosse needed employment so that she returned home her face "radiant," that the man from the city who intended marrying Eloise Ruelle was an innocent dupe while Eloise, the villager, is vicious.

Professor Dragland's assertions lack force.

If they have any force at all, it is only if we understand Scott to be presenting what on the surface appears to be an idyll. Only if the book seems to be an idyll, as all critics took it to be until 1973, can Professor Dragland attempt to show Scott undermining the genre with the irony of swamp and city motifs and so on and so forth. Only if the idyllic is dominant can there be beneath it an "ironic underside."

Professor Dragland promptly goes on to say:

> In Viger there is as much tragedy as we are likely to encounter in less idyllic surroundings. And not only the tragedy of circumstance we find in "Sedan" or the tragedy of hereditary weakness examined in "The Desjardins" or

"Paul Farlotte." There is also the tragedy caused by human nature, which Scott knew could be "sharp" as well as "genial" (the terms are from the opening poem).

Here Professor Dragland's arguments would seem to falter. If the book does *not* present itself as idyll, then there can be no artificiality for Scott to puncture. If the stories are *openly* 'tragic', Scott doesn't need to be 'ironic' to tip us off to the presence of tragedy.

The case that Professor Dragland makes for Scott's "irony" – and therefore for his "realism" and modernity – is painfully thin. His claim that the settings of "Sedan" and "The Bobolink" are ironic is simply another instance of zealous misreading. Equally thin is his case for Scott's use of "structural links" between the stories; "the image of a bird, caged or free," is, claims Professor Dragland, "variously significant" in five of the stories. *Variously* significant indeed. The motif of the city also provides, he claims, a structural link between the stories. As does – yes – the motif of the swamp.

But wobbly and ramshackle as it obviously is, Professor Dragland's introduction held considerable appeal. He had discovered – or invented – a new ancestor. He had extended the length of our indigenous tradition. And his reference to "structural links" between the stories would be seized on by others and pumped with ludicrous vigour.

BEFORE GOING ON to examine subsequent criticism of *In the Village of Viger* it might be interesting and salutary to change the focus for a moment. All this talk of irony and realism and modernity in Canada in 1896 should not make us lose perspective.

By 1883 Henry James had collected his fiction to that point in fourteen volumes. In 1897 he published *The Spoils of Poynton* and *What Maisie Knew*. Thomas Hardy released *Jude the Obscure* in 1895. In 1894 he had published the story collection *Life's Little Ironies*. Conrad published *An Outcast of the Islands* in 1896 and in 1897 *The Nigger of the "Narcissus"*. Kipling published *Many Inven-*

tions in 1893 and *The Jungle Books* in 1894 and 1895. *Kim* appeared in 1901. Oscar Wilde published *The Importance of Being Earnest* in 1895. Saki published the story collection *Reginald* in 1904.

In 1884 – twelve years before the appearance of *In the Village of Viger* – Mark Twain had published *Adventures of Huckleberry Finn*.

ONE OF THE FIRST post-Dragland references to *In the Village of Viger* comes in 1980 in a profile of Duncan Campbell Scott written by Professor D.M.R. Bentley for Volume I of the series *Profiles in Canadian Literature*. At the conclusion of his essay, Professor Bentley writes: "I am grateful to Stan Dragland for his valuable comments and suggestions during the preparation of this profile."

Professor Bentley offers the following assessment of Scott's fiction:

> Although Scott is primarily remembered as a poet, he did not by any means restrict himself to the writing of poetry. Two volumes of short-stories, *In the Village of Viger* and *The Witching of Elspie*, attest to his achievements as a writer of short fiction. Broadly speaking, Scott's short-stories fall into the category of local colour writing, which is to say writing which seeks, through the use of such techniques as realistic detail and regional dialect, to capture the flavour of a particular area and its people – in Scott's case primarily Quebec and the French-Canadians. (Incidentally, Scott is not alone in Canadian literature in depicting the life of a fictional village; his Viger has its equivalents in such places as Margaret Laurence's Manawaka and Alice Munro's Jubilee.)

This is the first reference I can find which links Scott, however obliquely, with modern writers. Was this linkage the invention of Professor Bentley, I wonder, or of Professor Dragland?

Also in 1980 appeared *The Penguin Book of Canadian Short*

Stories edited by Wayne Grady. Grady's credentials for editing such an important book were a degree in journalism, some years of freelance newspaper work, and a job as Managing Editor of *Books in Canada.* He has now, I understand, found his level working for *Harrowsmith,* a magazine which concerns itself with husbandry and mulch.

No one has, to my knowledge, commented on Grady's preface to the anthology. It is an amazing piece of work. It is little more than a nationalist manifesto crammed with bizarre assumptions, half-digested knowledge, and half-baked claims for Duncan Campbell Scott and his alleged influence.

Grady writes:

> Although short stories have been with us since Gilgamesh and the Book of Ruth, most theorists of the genre agree that the modern or literary short story was invented simultaneously by Edgar Allan Poe (1809-1849) in the United States and Nikolai Gogol (1809-1852) in Russia: in the words of Dostoevsky, 'We all spring from Gogol's "Overcoat."' In Canada we were writing short fiction before we wrote novels: *The History of Emily Montague* (1769) by Frances Brooke is generally recognized as the first Canadian novel, but it *is* epistolary, and it is not a far imaginative leap from composing letters to fictional friends to writing fictional letters to newspaper editors. As David Arnason has noted in his *Nineteenth Century Canadian Stories,* the Canadian short story can be considered as 'the development of the Letter to the Editor as a specialized literary form.' It was in such newspapers and magazines as the *Acadian Recorder,* in which Thomas McCulloch's 'Stepsure Letters' appeared in 1821, Joseph Howe's *Novascotian,* which first published Haliburton's Clockmaker series in 1837, and John Lovell's *Literary Garland,* which carried Susanna Moodie's 'Canadian Sketches' in 1847, that the modern Canadian short story was conceived.
>
> From its conception in pioneer journalism the Canadian

short story inherited in turn its most characteristic feature: a realism so intimate and natural that what it describes is often mistaken for real life. Robert McDougall, in his introduction to the New Canadian Library edition of *The Clockmaker*, informs us that 'when Haliburton visited England in 1838, Lord Abinger is reported to have raised himself on one elbow from a sick-bed long enough to ask the author if it was not true (as he firmly believed) "that there is a veritable Sam Slick in the flesh now selling clocks to the Bluenoses."' Similarly, Stephen Leacock's 'Sunshine Sketches' of small-town Ontario, first published in the Montreal *Star* in 1912, were so transparently modelled on the town of Orillia – to the point of using real names – that Leacock's biographer, David M. Legate, asserts that the humorist 'was extremely lucky to escape legal actions,' and certain prudent alterations were made in the book edition. And the 'semi-autobiographical' nature of works by such contemporary authors as Mordecai Richler, Margaret Laurence, and Alice Munro is often emphasized by critics, and sometimes by the authors themselves: Hugh Hood, for example, has referred to certain of his stories as 'semi-documentaries.'

The Canadian short story as a literary art form wasn't born, however, until 1896, with the publication of Duncan Campbell Scott's *In the Village of Viger*. If one thinks of Gogol and Poe as the twin parents of the modern short story – Poe representing the imaginative, fantastic side of the family, Gogol sticking closer to earth – then Scott's collection of ten realistic short stories about the residents of an ordinary French Canadian town is the salient indication of the branch the Canadian story was to follow. In that sense, at least, Canadian literature has had more in common with Russian literature than with American literature. *In the Village of Viger*, as a series of thematically linked short stories, looks back to Gogol's *Evenings Near the Village of Dikanka* – though with obvious nods in passing to Flaubert and de Maupassant – and ahead to Leacock's *Sunshine Sketches of a*

Little Town, Margaret Laurence's *A Bird in the House,* and Alice Munro's *Who Do You Think You Are?.* Scott is what the genealogists would call a gateway ancestor.

Grady obviously desires to give the modern Canadian story a pedigree and an indigenous tradition. He here proclaims as fact what Professor Solecki is rather tentatively implying. Grady claims that "the modern Canadian short story was conceived" in newspapers and magazines dating back to 1821. In other words, Grady is claiming an unbroken Canadian tradition.

This claim is flatly ludicrous; it presupposes a Canada hermetically sealed off from the USA and England.

Having asserted this tradition, Grady goes on to claim that the Canadian short story inherited from pioneer journalism its characteristic feature – "a realism so intimate and natural that what it describes is often taken for real life." He claims as writing within this inherited tradition of realism Leacock, Richler, Hood, Margaret Laurence, and Alice Munro. Grady has obviously not given much thought to what the word 'tradition' means; he ignores the possibility that the Canadian Hood could have been more influenced by the Italian Dante than he might have been by *The Orillia Intelligencer and Weekly Record.* He also has odd ideas about what constitutes 'realism'. Margaret Laurence perhaps comes closer than the others. But Richler with his gallery of caricatures? Leacock's not-so-sunny satire? Hood with stories which often have the shape of parable and *exemplum?* Alice Munro's dreamlike stories with their shifting times and changing points of view and haunting poetic images?

Grady obviously sees 'realism' as a good thing: 'realism' connects, so he claims, with the tradition of Russian Gogol whereas 'the fantastic' connects with the tradition of American Poe – and as a good Canadian Cultural Nationalist Grady would rather be connected with Outer Mongolia than with the USA.

It's difficult to know how to react to his claim that in its preference for 'realism' Canadian literature has more in common with Russian literature than with American. Drivel is perhaps better ignored. Yet this drivel *is* internationally distributed and Grady might be thought by readers outside Canada as being some sort of authority here. Unless, that is, they'd read some Russian literature of the nineteenth century.

I suppose that if Grady considers the ten stories in Scott's *In the Village of Viger* as "realistic," he's likely to respond in the same way to the Ukrainian folk tales in *Evenings Near the Village of Dikanka* – despite the fact that Gogol's stories are derived from folklore and from the Ukrainian equivalent of Punch and Judy shows and involve water nymphs, witches, night journeys on brooms, unholy spirits, lazy husbands with shrewish wives, scheming gypsies... *Evenings Near the Village of Dikanka* exhibits much the same degree of 'realism' as does *Fiddler on the Roof.*

And I suppose if we are to think of Gogol as "realistic," we'll have to forget his wonderful surrealism and grotesque farce; we'll have to forget "The Nose" and "The Overcoat" with Akaky's vengeful ghost.

Grady's account of *In the Village of Viger* is a major escalation from Professor Dragland's more tentative suggestions. Where Professor Dragland asserts an "ironic underside" to the pastoral which hints at "realism," Grady simply refers to the book as "Scott's collection of ten realistic short stories about the residents of an ordinary French Canadian town." Where Professor Dragland had referred, rather uneasily, to "structural links between the stories," Grady refers to the book as "a series of thematically linked short stories." Grady, in a major new development, claims the book as the forerunner of other collections of linked stories – collections by Leacock, Margaret Laurence, and Alice Munro. Finally, he claims Scott as "a gateway ancestor" – i.e. one through whom we have all passed, one from whom we are commonly descended.

For seventy-seven years, *In the Village of Viger* had been considered a collection of "local colour sketches." Within seven short years of Professor Dragland's introduction, criticism had elevated the book to being the founding and central text in the history of the short story in Canada. Further, Grady claims the book as the forerunner in a form claimed to be characteristically Canadian – the collection of linked stories.

(This is hinted at but not stated in Professor Bentley's 1980 comments quoted earlier on Margaret Laurence and Alice Munro.)

In 1983 Robert Weaver wrote the entry "Short Stories in English" for *The Oxford Companion to Canadian Literature.* His comment on Scott was as follows:

> ... in this period the most important collection, as a work of literature, was the poet Duncan Campbell Scott's *In the Village of Viger* (Boston, 1896), a series of stories that in a quiet, superbly controlled manner create the sense of a whole community.

No hint here of "ironic underside."

Weaver goes on:

> A decade and a half later (in 1912) another enduring collection of stories appeared: Stephen Leacock's *Sunshine Sketches of a Little Town.* Like Scott's book, and like so many other Canadian collections by a single author that would come later, *Sunshine Sketches* is a series of connected stories unified above all by setting, in this case the fictional Ontario town of Mariposa (Orillia).

And later in the entry, he writes:

> Collections of linked stories, which sometimes have a weight and narrative interest lacking in books of unconnected stories, are not a Canadian discovery. Probably the seminal book of this kind is Turgenev's series of lyrical stories about the Russian countryside, *Sketches from a Hunter's Album* (the title used for the Penguin Classics edition), published in 1852; its North American equivalent may be Sherwood Anderson's *Winesburg, Ohio* (1919). In

Canada, Scott's early *In the Village of Viger* and Leacock's *Sunshine Sketches* have been succeeded by, among other unified collections, Margaret Laurence's *A Bird in the House* (1970), stories about growing up in small-town Manitoba; Alice Munro's *Lives of Girls and Women* (1971), about growing up in small-town Ontario; George Elliott's *The Kissing Man* (1962), also about small-town Ontario; Jack Hodgins' *The Barclay Family Theatre* (1981) and earlier books [sic], which bring a mythic significance to life on Vancouver Island; and W.P. Kinsella's stories about baseball and about life on an Indian reserve in southern Alberta.

Weaver is more circumspect than Grady in urging the centrality of "linked stories" in Canadian literature. He has chosen a different Russian ancestor for the form – not Gogol but the conventionally accepted Turgenev. It's also interesting to note that Weaver is less chauvinistic than Grady and acknowledges the importance of Sherwood Anderson.

But Weaver's literary history is ambiguous if not shifty:

Probably the seminal book of this kind is Turgenev's ... *Sketches from a Hunter's Album* ... published in 1852; its North American equivalent may be Sherwood Anderson's *Winesburg, Ohio* (1919). In Canada, Scott's early *In the Village of Viger* and Leacock's *Sunshine Sketches* have been succeeded by ... other unified collections....

Weaver seems to be drawing a distinction between 'North America' and 'Canada' and seems to be implying that while *Winesburg, Ohio* is seminal for a North America which *really* means the USA only, *In the Village of Viger* is seminal for a Canada which is distinct from the USA and seemingly not in debt to Anderson. *Winesburg, Ohio* is a monument in the development of the modern story and to suggest that Scott's confection has comparable status reveals want of judgement. When Weaver describes *In the Village of Viger* as "early," he is presumably implying that *because the book predates*

Anderson it is Canada's 'seminal book.' This is simple silliness.

Weaver is less forthright than Grady in the question of Scott's influence on later writers but the implication is strong in his ambiguous "have been succeeded by ..."; Scott's 'successors' are, according to Weaver, Margaret Laurence, Alice Munro, George Elliott, Jack Hodgins, and W.P. Kinsella.

Weaver's contention that collections of linked stories "sometimes have a weight and narrative interest lacking in books of unconnected stories" strikes me as dubious and faintly philistine.

The entry on Duncan Campbell Scott in *The Oxford Companion to Canadian Literature* was written by George Wicken and swallows whole the Dragland Party Line. Indeed, it is difficult to avoid the suspicion that Wicken's glib paragraph is based more on Professor Dragland's introduction to *In the Village of Viger* than on acquaintance with the actual text.

Wicken writes:

> *In the Village of Viger,* set in nineteenth-century Québec, details the lives of both the villagers and those whose lives are intertwined with them. Although the characters are more appropriate to romance than to realism (a shoemaker, a pedler, an aristocrat fallen on hard times), there is a degree of realism in these stories that is uncommon in the short fiction of the 1890s: encroaching upon the idyllic village are the forces of industrialization and urbanization. As Stan Dragland has pointed out in his introduction to the 1973 reprint of *In the Village of Viger,* the village is in danger of being swallowed by the metropolis of which it is one of the 'outlying wards'. In examining a closed society being penetrated by forces that threaten to disrupt its unity, Scott is being consistent with the themes he explores in his Indian poetry.

To describe this book as an examination of "a closed society being penetrated by forces that threaten to disrupt its unity" is a grotesque misrepresentation of its contents. *In the Village of Viger* is not an 'examination' of anything at all; it has no sociological focus whatsoever; it is a collection of sentimental and melodramatic tales.

What forces are 'penetrating' Viger?

Things from the swamp, perhaps.

Could it possibly be described as quibbling to point out that Wicken hasn't even managed to read correctly the first page of the first story in the book? Viger is *not* one of the city's outlying wards; how on earth could one have what Wicken calls an "idyllic village" as a city ward? What Scott *actually* wrote was: "But when the time came for Viger to be mentioned in the city papers as one of the outlying wards, what a change there would be! There would be no unfenced fields...."

Yet one can see *why* Dragland and Wicken wish to replace Scott's book with one of their own invention. 'Industrialization' and 'urbanization' destroying the 'organic' unity of the rural is so much more trendy and relevant and *chic* than having to deal with dated tales written in an English which manages to be both stilted and overblown.

Sober examination of the book reveals that all the 'industrialization' and 'urbanization' and 'motif-of-the-city' stuff derives from the first two pages of the first story in the collection, "The Little Milliner," and from nowhere else – a narrow and perilous base for such a towering superstructure as Professor Dragland and subsequent critics attempt to rear.

The Oxford Companion to Canadian Literature appeared in 1983. Two years later the Dragland Line and the Weaver Line were conflated and inflated by J.R. (Tim) Struthers in his article on Canadian short fiction in *The Canadian Encyclopedia*.

It is worth noting that Struthers' 1982 Ph.D. dissertation on Canadian story cycles was supervised by none other than Professor Stan Dragland.

Struthers writes:

Scott's work looks back to 19th-century American gothic and romantic and local-colour writing, yet its ironic tone connects it with mid-20th-century writing, and his use of imagery anticipates the poetically conceived short stories written later in the century. Moreover, as a unit, *In the Village of Viger* is a foundation stone in the Canadian tradition of the story cycle.

Struthers states flatly what Professor Dragland and Robert Weaver advance a touch more cautiously. Here "ironic underside" has become "ironic tone" – a firmer and rather different statement. This "ironic tone," claims Struthers, connects Scott's work with mid-twentieth century writing. And Professor Dragland's vague suggestion that there exists between the stories "a rhythm of structural links" – whatever *that* might mean – involving "the image of a bird, caged or free," is here inflated to a "use of imagery [which] anticipates the poetically conceived short stories written later in the century."

(No examples of this "use of imagery" offered.)

Of his three assertions concerning possible connections between Scott's book and later writing, the first two are flatly untrue while the last is more than debatable. This is myth-making in action. Struthers is here visibly inventing an indigenous tradition and a canon.

He continues:

[Margaret Laurence's] story cycle *A Bird in the House* (1970) stands with Scott's *In the Village of Viger*, Leacock's *Sunshine Sketches of a Little Town* and Hood's *Around the Mountain* as major benchmarks for subsequent creators of story cycles (or sketchbooks) in Canada. Munro's first book of stories, *Dance of the Happy Shades* (1968), contained the best of her work from nearly 2 decades. By the early 1980s, Munro had the best popular and international reputation of Canadian short story writers. She emerged as the writer most often identified with the rebirth of the Canadian short story, and as the writer most prominently concerned with trying to shape short stories into coherent books or story cycles – most notably in *Who Do You Think You Are?* (1978).

Notice that *In the Village of Viger* has now been described as "a foundation stone" and as one of the "major benchmarks for subsequent creators of story cycles (or sketchbooks) in Canada." Notice that the distinction between 'story' and 'sketch' is being fudged so that Hood – a subject of Struthers' continuing interest and study – can be enshrined in the pantheon. Notice how Alice Munro's popularity and international reputation are stressed so that her one "coherent" book of stories will shed added lustre on "the Canadian tradition of the story cycle." Notice, too, that the words "most notably in" mean 'only in'.

We will return to this idea of tradition shortly.

ONE OF THE FEW Canadian literary critics whose work seems to me, in the main, sensitive and reliable is W.J. Keith who in 1985 published a literary history entitled *Canadian Literature in English*. I was interested to read his comments on Scott's fiction and was particularly interested by what he did *not* say. There is no mention in what follows of ironic underside, ironic tone, imagery, structural links, realism, tradition, or ancestors gateway or otherwise.

Some of the best fictional writing in the twentieth century has employed the short-story form, and here again the nineteenth-century examples seem little more than pale shadows of the later achievement. The more popular collections of the period, like Gilbert Parker's *Pierre and His People* (1892) and E.W. Thompson's *Old Man Savarin* (1895), relied for the most part on thrilling or sentimental plots and homely characterization, and now seem stereotyped and obvious to modern readers. Although sharing in these qualities, one collection escapes their limitations through its stylistic lucidity and technical expertise. This is D.C. Scott's

In the Village of Viger (1896). Scott offers the stories in Arcadian or pastoral terms, but in fact they vary radically in tone from the tender and idyllic to the Gothic and sombre. All are unified by their setting in a rural French-Canadian village portrayed with humour but without condescension, and by the quiet but firm control of Scott's narration. Each story is absorbing in itself, but together they build up a convincing sense of a particular communal life with recurring characters, a consistent background, and an emotional atmosphere that alters with the mood of each story but remains stable in terms of the whole book. Scott devoted most of his creative energies to poetry, and in later years only fitfully exercised his talents for short fiction, but his contribution was important historically in that it demonstrated the virtues of care and finish in a form that hitherto had rarely been approached with artistic seriousness.

I do rather part company with Keith when he says the stories "together ... build up a convincing sense of a particular communal life with recurring characters, a consistent background, and an emotional atmosphere that alters with the mood of each story but remains stable in terms of the whole book." The last part of that sentence is vague to the point of being verbal sleight-of-hand but I *am* puzzled by Keith's being convinced of Viger's communal life. Weaver, too, spoke of "the sense of a whole community."

Is the background consistent? *Do* the characters recur?

I am unable to gain much sense of Viger as a place and strongly doubt that Scott had a picture in his mind of the layout of the village. Could one draw even the roughest map of Viger from the information given us? How many people live in Viger? If Eloise Ruelle lives at No. 68, how long are the streets? How many banks did the village support? How many taverns? No one seems to have commented on the fact that the Viger suggested by background detail in "The Tragedy of the Seigniory" seems a Viger utterly different from the Viger of "The Bobolink."

And "recurring characters"? Out of thirty-three named characters, only two appear in more than one story. Monsieur Cuerrier appears in two stories and the Widow Laroque appears in two stories and is mentioned in two others. While it's *technically* accurate to speak of "recurring characters," it does give a severely misleading impression.

I am far less persuaded than Keith and Weaver of Viger's "communal life" and remain baffled by Keith's praise of Scott's "stylistic lucidity and technical expertise"; the suspicion is beginning to grow in me that their enthusiasm results simply from their having had the intestinal fortitude to read *Pierre and His People* while I didn't, haven't, and won't.

The year following the appearance of W.J. Keith's *Canadian Literature in English*, Margaret Atwood and Robert Weaver compiled *The Oxford Book of Canadian Stories* (1986). Each contributed a separate introduction. Margaret Atwood's is of some interest; she seems to have retreated in recent years from her earlier extreme nationalism:

> What, if anything, distinguishes a 'Canadian' short story from one of any other kind? Individually considered, probably nothing. There is no essence of Canada that, sprinkled on a piece of prose fiction, will magically transform it. A Canadian short story may or may not be set in the frozen North or trackless wilderness and contain snow, beavers, Mounties, Inuit, or dead animals, but these days the odds are against it; Mounties in particular have become somewhat scarce. Nor is the place of origin of the writer any necessary clue. Twelve per cent of Canada's population was not born there. Several of the writers in this collection first saw the light of day elsewhere; several spent their childhoods here but now live in other countries. The definition of 'Canadian short story', like that of 'Canadian' itself, has a hard core with fuzzy edges. Nor is style an indication: Canadian short-story writers are now as eclectic in their approach as

story writers elsewhere in the English-speaking world.

This sounds sensible and promising.

But what she offers with one hand she tries to hold onto with the other:

> But several forms of short prose narrative were written before people got around to talking about art, and I like to think that the Canadian short story owes something to them, as recent poetry certainly does. These were the explorers' journals, which were naturally episodic, and the later travellers' accounts, such as Anna Jameson's, and descriptions of the country, such as Susanna Moodie's and Joseph Howe's, which also contain many 'character sketches' and short narrative episodes. The short story in Québec draws from the *fabliau* and from the oral fairy-tale traditions there, and that of English Canada has frequently made use of its own oral forms, the tall tale or yarn, the local – usually scandalous or supernatural – legend, and the joke. The Jamesian psychological study and the Zolaesque slice of life are only two of the Canadian short story's many forbears.

We see here another sad and wistful attempt to connect the modern Canadian story with "oral forms" and "explorers' journals" and "the joke" – an attempt to establish or invent, in other words, an indigenous Canadian tradition.

In the "Biographical Notes" on the authors at the back of the book, Weaver and Margaret Atwood write:

> Scott published two collections of short stories, *In the Village of Viger* (1896) and *The Witching of Elspie* (1923), both of which have influenced the development of the short story in Canada. *In the Village of Viger* – linked nostalgic tales of life in a quiet village near Montreal – was the precursor of similar collections by Leacock, Margaret Laurence, Alice

Munro, Jack Hodgins, Edna Alford, Sandra Birdsell, and others.

In 1983 in *The Oxford Companion to Canadian Literature* Weaver had written that *In the Village of Viger* had "been succeeded by ... other unified collections." Here, he and Margaret Atwood use the word "precursor" which is more forceful but still cleverly ambiguous. However, it should be noted that the sentence containing the word "precursor" follows a sentence which claims that *In the Village of Viger* has "influenced the development of the short story in Canada." The claim that is being made seems clear. The list of those claimed as being in the 'tradition' of *In the Village of Viger* is longer than the list Weaver had compiled in 1983; added to the 'tradition' now are Edna Alford, Sandra Birdsell, and "others."

Any reader who has had the patience to follow thus far the critical fortunes of *In the Village of Viger* must by now believe that further inflation of the book would be impossible.

Any reader would be wrong.

SCOTT'S REPUTATION swelled to bursting point in 1987 when Professor W.H. New published a book called *Dreams of Speech and Violence: The Art of the Short Story in Canada and New Zealand.* In his history of the short story in Canada, one of his section headings is "*D.C. Scott's Revolution, 1820-1920*"; the revolution to which he is referring is the revolution which led to 'realism' in Canadian fiction. Professor New advances startling claims for *In the Village of Viger* suggesting that Scott occupies a position in the history of fiction in Canada comparable with the dominant position held in New Zealand writing by Katherine Mansfield.

It is difficult to convey how heavily Professor New freights Scott's little story book with meaning. In essence, Professor New entirely accepts everything that Professor Dragland says about 'irony' and 'city and swamp motifs' and goes on from there to see in these tales moral, psychological, and historical intentions of such complexity and profundity that after each daunting paragraph I'm left whispering to myself:

... 'strewth!

The following quotation will perhaps suggest something of the complexity both of Professor New's argument and of his prose:

> When Stan Dragland in 1973 wrote the introduction to the New Canadian Library edition of *In the Village of Viger and Other Stories* (the extended title indicates the inclusion of seven of Scott's later stories in a section appended to this reprint of *Viger*), he confirmed what occasional anthologists like Raymond Knister, Roberto Ruberto, and Giose Rimanelli had earlier declared: that the force of Scott's stories derived from their realism. And he drew attention to some of the ways the text challenges the very notions of pastoral perfection which other critics had presumed it to represent. By image, Dragland reveals, Scott invites readers to respond to the realities that underlie the illusions of orderly permanence:
>
> Viger is a village in transition: 'New houses had already commenced to spring up in all directions, and there was a large influx of the labouring population which overflows from large cities.' This sentence comes from the opening paragraphs of 'The Little Milliner' which not only set the scene for that story but introduce an urban undercurrent which surfaces several times in the volume ...
>
> Swamp and city motifs are part of the ironic underside of pastoral Viger, and would tip the reader off to the presence in Viger of something more than the pleasant relief from our cares that Scott promises in his opening poem, even if there were no other irony in the book.
>
> In fact, some of the settings are ironic, like the situation of the Arbique Inn in 'Sedan': 'There was something idyllic

about this contented spot; it seemed to be removed from the rest of the village, to be on the boundaries of Arcadia, the first inlet to its pleasant dreamy field' [sic]. The key word is 'seemed' ...

Two of Dragland's key words are 'undercurrent' and 'underside.' Elsewhere in his introduction, 'understatement' is a third. Dragland uses these terms to describe Scott's realism but they suggest something more as well: that Scott was aware of hidden faces and submerged motivations, and that he used language with deliberate subversive indirectness in order to reveal the truth behind linguistic and social conventions. In Viger, neither temporal nor social order is permanent; all that lasts are time and change, both of which require the characters to respond to the alternatives their lives present them with. They can embrace them, live with them, or explain them away in myth and mystery. But they must contend. And both thematically and structurally, their ways of contending shape a pattern of fictional discourse through which Scott's insights into social behaviour amount to more than mere glosses on the surface charms of an imagined country life.

At a simple thematic level, these alternatives are both political and psychological. The stories tell of the political enmities of the Franco-Prussian War in 'Sedan' and of private battles for power: Eloise Ruelle's callous manipulations in 'No. 68 Rue Alfred de Musset' and Mme Laroque's wars with her rivals in fashion and love, Mlle Viau in 'The Little Milliner' and Césarine Angers in 'The Wooing of Monsieur Cuerrier.' They tell also of the villagers' psychological fear of outsiders, as in 'The Pedler'; of their failure to recognize the stranger as their own as in 'The Tragedy of the Seigniory'; of the madness they suppress, as in 'The Desjardins,' and the madness that others must contain, as in 'Paul Farlotte.' And they tell of blindness and dream, the companions of insight and practicality, as in 'The Bobolink' and

'Josephine Labrosse.' Always the characters live with this companion otherness, this extra dimension of themselves which they scarcely recognize, yet which affects them variously with conflict or with grace. And from his observations of their behaviour under stress, Scott teases his cumulative portrait of a whole way of life facing change, finding eloquence in the moment of passing and challenge in the moment at hand.

Internally, the particular themes overlap – 'Sedan,' for example, concerns love, family, jealousy, prejudice, and the motivations for love and enmity in general, not the Franco-Prussian war alone – and such themes, like the recurrent images of birds encaged and in flight, tie the stories together by motif. More broadly, the thematic pattern invites the reader to perceive the social and moral ramifications of the notion of a synchronic alternative self ...

... 'strewth!

My experience of reading *In the Village of Viger* is obviously quite unlike Professor New's experience. I am bewildered – even dazed – by his baroque commentaries on these simple tales. All I can suggest to an interested reader is to read the story "Sedan" with great care; if a reader writes to me saying he or she genuinely feels that "the thematic pattern invites the reader to perceive the social and moral ramifications of the notion of a synchronic alternative self," I will gladly and publicly eat Professor New's hat.

LET US PAUSE now and recapitulate.

Since 1973, the reputation among academics and cultural nationalists of *In the Village of Viger* has changed dramatically. From being a book almost unknown, it is now being talked about as the central and founding text in Canadian short fiction. Scott has an importance within our literature, it is claimed, comparable with the importance in American literature of Sherwood Ander-

son and comparable with the importance in New Zealand literature of Katherine Mansfield.

Modern writers, it is said, have been influenced by Scott; he is
our "gateway ancestor," according to Grady, from whom we are
all descended. Margaret Atwood and Weaver claim that *In the
Village of Viger* "influenced the development of the short story in
Canada."

Struthers in his article in *The Canadian Encyclopedia* claims *In
the Village of Viger* as "a foundation stone in the Canadian tradition
of the story cycle."

Professor D.M.R. Bentley hinted that Margaret Laurence and
Alice Munro were in the tradition of the story cycle which was
founded by Scott. Grady cites Leacock, Margaret Laurence, and
Alice Munro. Weaver in 1983 claims Leacock, Margaret
Laurence, Alice Munro, George Elliott, Jack Hodgins, and W.P.
Kinsella. Struthers claims Margaret Laurence, Hugh Hood, and
Alice Munro. Weaver and Margaret Atwood in 1986 add to
Weaver's previous list now claiming Edna Alford, Sandra
Birdsell, and "others."

All of these claims and assertions are nonsense.

Scott had a very limited contemporary reputation. How can he
be our "gateway ancestor" if virtually no one had read his book?
How can Scott hold a comparable position with Anderson and
Katherine Mansfield if he is unknown in our society? How can *In
the Village of Viger* have "influenced the development of the short
story in Canada" if between 1896 and 1945 *the book simply was not
available to be read?* And why, in the twenty-five years after 1945,
when perhaps 350 copies of the book were sold, why should we
imagine that young writers then would be stylistically influenced
by a book that was a period piece from a distant era?

The present reputation of *In the Village of Viger* stems from the
desire of various academics and cultural nationalists to be the
possessors of a tradition; lacking one, they simply *invented* one.
No one in the lackadaisical world of Canadian literary studies
batted an eyelid. No one seems to notice, no one seems to care

that our literature is being raised on a foundation of ignorance, incompetence, self-deception, and lies. The same sort of thing is happening with other texts. The situation *should* be causing alarm.

The origins of this new 'tradition' can be traced directly to Professor Stan Dragland's introduction to the New Canadian Library edition of *In the Village of Viger*. The main ideas of this 'tradition' are now accepted as fact. They are embedded in *The Canadian Encyclopedia* and are thereby given respectability and currency.

"... the Canadian tradition of the story cycle ..."

WE'RE AT A FASCINATING point in our literary history. Nearly every writer of any importance in our history is still alive and on the phone. This situation will not last much longer. Having become intrigued by the sheer nerve of the "story cycle" invention and knowing most of the writers for whom Scott is supposed to have been a "precursor," I decided to phone them all and ask them without prior conversation if they'd ever read *In the Village of Viger*.

Hugh Hood, Alice Munro, Sandra Birdsell, Edna Alford, W.P. Kinsella, George Elliott, and Jack Hodgins.

Of these seven writers cited as being in the tradition, not a single one had read the book. Not a single one had *heard* of it.

Hugh Hood said: "I would actively resent any association of my name with *In the Village of Viger*."

Alice Munro said: "Tell them that the book that influenced me was *Winesburg, Ohio*."

Sandra Birdsell said that her main influences were Sherwood Anderson, Flannery O'Connor, and – most interestingly – Alice Munro.

Edna Alford had never heard of the book.

Nor had W.P. Kinsella.

Nor had George Elliott.

"Was he the one," said Jack Hodgins, "who wrote stories about bears and – was it wolves?"

"I don't think so," I said. "I think from the sound of it that was G.D. Whatsisname."

Jack Hodgins went on to say that for him as a child in British Columbia, Scott in Ottawa would have been as foreign as a writer in Mexico – and just as far away. He also said that he thought the traditions of most Canadian writers were not Canadian at all, that most Canadian literary traditions were invented by academics retroactively.

Six

WHEN I WAS EXPLAINING to Edna Alford why I'd wanted to know if she'd read *In the Village of Viger*, I told her Scott was being compared in importance with Katherine Mansfield and she interrupted me saying:

"Oh! Katherine Mansfield! Yes! Yes!"

This leads to my next point. When Professor Solecki says that I have a "problematic relationship to literary tradition," what he *means* is that I have a problematic relationship with the particular 'tradition' that *he* has invented and defined as 'Canadian'.

Most academic thinking in Canada about the nature of Canadian literary tradition is distorted and confused by nationalist desire. Because Writer A is a Canadian, the thinking seems to go, then Writer B who is also a Canadian must stand in a relationship to Writer A. The further assumption has to be made that Writers A and B remain largely uninfluenced by any writing from outside Canada's borders so that the putative connections between them remain unmuddied by non-Canadian matter. This is the vision that Professor Solecki offers when he talks, uneasily, about writers brought up "on *Wacousta* and back issues of *The Canadian Forum*." I am often accused of being anti-Canadian for maintaining that literary tradition does not work in such simple ways. Nationalist critics are attempting to impose straight lines of influence and descent on what is by nature as wiggly, tangled, slippery, and international as a colander of spaghetti.

One of my first vivid literary experiences – a Paul on the Damascus road experience – was with Jaroslav Hasek's *The Good Soldier Schweik*. Later, when I was about seventeen or eighteen, I remember being enraptured by the ineffable artistry of Hemingway's "Hills Like White Elephants." But somewhere between these two experiences I will never forget the crawl of my skin when I first heard the voice in Katherine Mansfield's "Miss Brill"; it affects me in much the same way still.

Three profound influences upon me as a writer, then, were a Czech-in-translation, a sort-of New Zealander, and an expatriate American. There were, of course, many others and I might cite Sherwood Anderson, Ring Lardner, Nathanael West, Eudora Welty, P.G. Wodehouse, Evelyn Waugh, Charles Dickens, my friends from Montreal Story Tellers – Ray Smith, Hugh Hood, and Clark Blaise – the oratory of my father's sermons and the tradition from which *that* derived, and a mess of other influences such as many of us have – radio and theatre and Biggles and Bulldog Drummond and everything back to the stories my mother used to read to me at night ... *the great grey-green, greasy Limpopo River, all set about with fever-trees....*

I do not consider my literary inheritance as in any way unusual.

It did not surprise me at all to hear that Katherine Mansfield is part of the personal tradition of Edna Alford, a Canadian writer in Livelong, Saskatchewan.

Why should it surprise anyone?

Nor was I surprised to hear that in Sandra Birdsell's tradition are Sherwood Anderson, Flannery O'Connor, and Alice Munro.

Nor *will* I be surprised to learn that some writer yet to publish from India or England or the deep South holds Alice Munro shining in his or her pantheon.

Writers in English are influenced by other writers in English. Writers are, by nature, receivers. Writers are not only influenced by others working in the same genre. 'Influence' and 'tradition' are infinitely complex. Surely most prose writers *must* be influenced by poets? I would imagine I owe as much to the Imagists and to Hopkins, Pound, Graves, Crowe Ransom, Newlove, and Larkin as I do to Hemingway or Katherine Mansfield. I've known writers who have claimed that the shape of their work is deeply influenced by other arts, by music, by painting, by architecture. And why not? The process of fertilization is endless.

The loyalty of good writers is to language. Writers seek out and honour the energy of language. A remark of the Canadian jazz musician Paul Bley says much about career and tradition in the arts: "You go where the heat is and then you *become* the heat."

Professor Solecki has said that I am trying "to recast the Canadian tradition" so that as an immigrant I'll be able to "have a place in it." But doesn't he find it odd that immigrant *and* native-born share the *same* tradition, that Sherwood Anderson and Katherine Mansfield are common currency?

Professor Solecki writes:

... by characterizing the best work of the past twenty-five years as modern or international in style Metcalf, consciously or unconsciously, leaves the Canadian writer and critic without a Canadian tradition.

Professor Solecki can relax; what he fears *will* happen actually *did* happen twenty-five years ago. Precisely what happened to Canadian poetry in the 1940s happened to Canadian prose in the 1960s. Does Professor Solecki feel that poetry written in Canada since the 1940s isn't Canadian because it embraced new American and British models? Does he feel that genuine *Canadian* poetry is that which existed *prior* to the 1940s – poetry which was largely a version of Victorian and Georgian British poetry?

Is British poetry after Pound and the Imagists and Eliot not really British?

The stories of Hugh Hood, Alice Munro, Clark Blaise, Ray Smith, Audrey Thomas, Kent Thompson, Edna Alford, Sandra Birdsell, Jack Hodgins, Keath Fraser, Norman Levine, and Leon Rooke are all written in a modern or international style.

Are these writers not Canadian?

In an earlier section, I quoted George Bowering. In the same letter, Bowering goes on to make what seem to me essential points about the nature of tradition and 'Canadian-ness'. He writes:

If one can say that the writing is Canadian as long as the writer is Canadian, that is fine with me. But the main problem, as I see it, is that Mathews and Co. have missed the main thing that has happened to the idea of tradition in the twentieth century, the main lesson of International Modernism. Before the twentieth century it might have been arguable that a person fell willy-nilly into some sort of linguo-national tradition.... But with Modernism, we were given the option of CHOOSING a tradition on individual or group terms. That we can decide to belong to, say, a naturalist or socialist tradition and place ourselves with Japanese and German and African writers and musicians etc. that we feel have been touched by similar international / class sympathies and interests. One can also be a little more determinist without being national: I agree with Sheila Watson who says that she felt that she was in a tradition that was formed by the intellectual environment during the time that she was becoming a fully-sentient person – so she is in a tradition that includes Wyndham Lewis, Eliot, etc. That seems simple and intelligent to me. Tradition is a word that comes from the same root as trade; and literature works as trade does, sometimes pan-oceanic.

And that seems simple and intelligent to me, too.
"The writing is Canadian as long as the writer is Canadian."
Yes.
And what is a Canadian?
There can only be one answer to that question. It is an answer that many Canadians do not wish to accept. A Canadian is a person who holds Canadian citizenship.

Seven

EACH OF THE MOST widely disseminated descriptions of Canadian literature appears to be staring steadfastly over its shoulder. Each seems intent on summing up, on drawing lines beneath the columns and closing the account. But Canadian literature is not ending. It has barely begun.

The last twenty-five years have seen the beginnings of serious writing here, not just an isolated book or two as in the past but enough good writing for us to begin to talk about the emergence of a literature. In another fifty or seventy-five years we might be able to begin to describe it. At the moment, we can't. At the moment, we can't even begin to describe a possible canon.

We are far too close in time to our writers to estimate their achievement and put them into perspective. Reputations are still shaking down. Bliss Carman once would have seemed an obvious contender for Canadian literary immortality. Not very long ago he had a large and popular audience; even Ezra Pound once thought him the only living "American" [sic] poet who "would not improve by drowning." Now he is chiefly cherished for such giggling bed-jinglers as:

> Make me over, Mother April,
> When the sap begins to stir!

E.J. Pratt, too, would have seemed at one time obviously secure. How important a poet was A.J.M. Smith? How genuinely funny was Leacock? And, by contrast, how underrated a poet is Irving Layton?

Each passing decade taps the literary kaleidoscope into a new configuration and design.

Writers who once seemed monumental and central are, as time passes, coming to be seen in a different perspective. Morley Callaghan's stock is tumbling. Sinclair Ross's reputation is increasingly problematic. The ghastliness of Ernest Buckler's prose is beginning to be more widely admitted. Hugh MacLennan is shrinking. Margaret Laurence, who once seemed at the centre of contemporary writing in Canada, is now seen as a more peripheral figure, a representative of the end of an older narrative tradition. Some of the stars that shone in the firmament of the seventies are now dimmed or extinct. Who reads Hugh Garner? Where now is Dave Godfrey? Does Rudy Wiebe still bestride our narrow stage?

On the other hand, some writers once ignored in the nationalist frenzy have been rehabilitated. Ethel Wilson's stock is steadily rising. Mavis Gallant was allowed back into the fold in 1978. Norman Levine seems to have been forgiven.

WHAT WILL THIS emerging literature of ours be like?

Everything militates against an inward-looking and nationalist literature. It is doubtful whether there will ever be new forms or new rhetorics that are distinctively Canadian. I suspect that Canadian literature, in the way that we've thought about it for the last fifty years, is fast disappearing. Falling sales, unit cost, the size of print runs – the mechanics and economics of the publishing industry are dictating change and the direction is outwards into the larger world. Penguin Books, for example, needs to print 7000 copies of a Canadian title in order to achieve economies of scale. In many cases, they cannot sell that many books in Canada and so must lay off at least 3000 of that 7000 in the USA, Australia, and England. Marketing problems and the diminishing audience are dictating internationalism as a matter of – if I may use the word – survival.

The relatively rapid appearance of literary agents has also changed the face and direction of Canadian writing. Young writers with agents now think automatically of publication throughout the English-speaking world. They no longer dream of being the best in Alberta; they dream of New York, London, and Paris. As the agents sell Canadian books in the USA, New York is becoming as familiar to Canadian writers as Toronto. It is inevitable, too, that as personal contacts between Canadian and American writers develop, the two literatures will move even closer together.

Our cultural nationalists fear that this will spell the end of the possibility of a literature distinctively Canadian. But being 'distinctively Canadian' is not, of course, a *literary* concern; it is political. It is possible to be 'distinctively Canadian' and thoroughly bad. Indeed, a writer's *intention* to be 'distinctively Canadian' almost ensures lugubrious awfulness.

In his essay "What Was Canadian Literature? Taking Stock of the CanLit Industry," T.D. MacLulich offers a classic exhibition of such nationalist fears and paranoia:

> Canadian literature, like Canadian culture generally, exists in a state of permanent crisis, always on the verge of being overwhelmed by outside forces. The term "Canadian literature" identifies a mixed category, whose specifications are partly literary and partly political. Whatever the literary purists among us may like to think, the justification for isolating Canadian literature as a separate field of study is linked with a conviction of our cultural divergence from the United States. Simply to assert that the Canadian tradition contains everything that Canadian writers have published or will produce is not good enough. If we read Canadian works in a purely esthetic or purely "literary" way, then we ignore – and in effect we deny – their Canadianness. We then have no reason for grouping them in a separate category, and we should just sprinkle them back into the general academic menu (some to thicken Modern Fiction, others to flavour Modern Poetry, and the remaining few to garnish Modern Drama).

Here again are the familiar themes. Why does MacLulich feel that it is "not good enough" to describe as Canadian those books written by Canadians? Because to be 'Canadian' a book must perform the political task of demonstrating "cultural divergence from the United States." Our books, poor things, must shoulder the burden of building Canadian Identity.

"Outside forces" are massing to overwhelm us. And how long have you felt this way, Professor MacLulich? I see. Yes. And you've experienced sleep disturbance, you say. And night sweating?

The one point MacLulich makes with which I'm in agreement is that Canadian literature "exists in a state of permanent crisis." That state of crisis, however, has nothing to do with "being overwhelmed by outside forces." "Outside forces" are not the problem at all. *Internal* forces are the problem. Canadian literature's permanent crisis is that there exist very few Canadians willing to read it.

The answer to this crisis is *not* to make patriotic appeals, to beg or blackmail people into 'reading Canadian'; that is what has always been done and it has always made the problem worse. It is the identification again of art with nationalism and it is always a mistake. To read a book because it is a Canadian book or a Saskatchewan book is to read with the wrong motivation. Reading should always be a private and a wayward pleasure.

I have for these reasons a strong mistrust of the growth of regionalism in our literature. Regionalism is simply a smaller, shriller version of nationalism. Aggressively regional audiences are provincial in the worst way. And provincial publishing is setting the sights deliberately low. MacLulich is, of course, a supporter of regionalism because he feels safer when the wagons are in a protective circle. He calls for "Resistance to the homogenizing tendency of international modernism." He calls for a fiction "rooted in local soil." If our fiction is not so rooted, "it will lose solidity and be blown away by whatever intellectual winds happen by."

When I was a misspent youth in England, jazz fans were split into two major camps. One group supported the revival of traditional New Orleans jazz while the more contemporary and musical camp was devoted to bop. Boppers referred to the trad fans with their antiquarian interests as 'mouldy figs'. Reading

MacLulich, the phrase has been much in my mind.

The division he is trying to create between "international modernism" and fiction "rooted in local soil" is an entirely false division. It would be difficult to imagine a book more rooted in local soil than Joyce's *Ulysses*. Did Joyce's modernism cause Dublin to "lose solidity"? Did Alice Munro's use of the tools of "international modernism" somehow weaken the rootedness of her vision of Jubilee?

When invited once to address a meeting of the Writers Guild of Alberta, I caused considerable coolness when I suggested that one had to mine international literature to find technical possibilities which could be assimilated and adapted to make Moose Creek real to the world. Alberta would not be celebrated by its writers talking only to each other; the world would not come to them. Their task was to take Moose Creek to the world. Oxford, Mississippi, was also once an unknown, one-horse town. Faulkner *lived* in Oxford, I reminded them, but he sure as hell didn't *publish* there.

But if regionalism *is* transitory and if the trend in our writing *is* generally outward and opening and if reputations *are* still shaking down and settling and if the cultural theorists *are* as patently dotty as the evidence suggests, then why waste time on taking our literature's temperature, on polemics such as this? Why not simply let time winnow wheat from chaff?

Were our literary culture like the literary cultures of the USA and England, I would feel perfectly content to leave all literary judgements to the mercy of time passing. But our literary culture is unlike others; it is an animal of a strange stripe, a sport among cultures.

CANADIAN LITERARY CULTURE dates, roughly speaking, from 1957 when The Canada Council was founded and it is almost entirely the creation of the State. It continues largely dependent on state subsidy. The State desires a literature because it seems to believe that a literature is one of the marks of a mature and civilized country and because it seems to believe that the possession of a literature will somehow unify us as a people and define our national identity. To these ends, the State has meddled in literary matters to the tune of hundreds of millions of dollars.

But these thirty years of massive subsidy have failed to secure an audience. In my 1987 pamphlet, *Freedom from Culture*, I wrote:

> A country's literature is not a collection of books. A country's literature is not contained in the holdings of the National Library. A country's literature cannot be represented by a paperback reprint series nor can Histories or Companions chart its depths and reaches.
> A literature is a relationship.
> A literature is a relationship between books and readers. It goes back into the past and looks towards the future. A literature is those books which readers hold in their hearts and minds. A literature is made up of those books which the collective readership through time loves and deems indispensable.

What books do Canadians hold in their hearts? What are the books that all Canadians have read and loved? What books from the Canadian past live on with us? What, simply put, are *our* books?

Wacousta?

Why *hasn't* a Canadian Literature come into being? Why, after thirty years of state encouragement and massive subsidy, is the literary relationship so attenuated and uncertain?

The sheer size of the subsidies and of their attendant bureaucracies combine to give the illusion of cultural health. Most people tend to assume that all must be well because books keep on appearing and are reviewed. Somewhere in Canada someone is always talking of 'culture' or 'cultural sovereignty'. Some huffer or puffer is always refusing to put on the free trade bargaining table with the Americans our subsidized cultural glories. But for all the massive grants to publishers and for all the chorus of croaking about 'culture', the unpalatable fact remains that a work of fiction, if well-reviewed, seems to sell, on average, 800-1200 copies.

William Hoffer, antiquarian bookseller and specialist in Canadian first editions, has claimed that the creation of The Canada Council in 1957 destroyed an emerging literature. One of his catalogues (List 60) contains the following entry:

Item 97.
Indian File Books. Toronto. McClelland and Stewart. 1948-1958.

Cloth and patterned paper over boards. Designed by Paul Arthur, the Managing Editor of *Here and Now*, typographically the most innovative and striking periodical of the 1940s, this series of more or less annual collections of the best poetry of each year was of colossal importance in the 1950s. These books are the mainstream against which Contact Press struggled, and if it had not been for The Canada Council, that struggle might have resulted in a serious literature in this country.

Indian File 1, DANIELLS (ROY) *Deeper into the Forest* (1948).
Indian File 2, FINCH (ROBERT) *The Strength of the Hills* (1948).
Indian File 3, REANEY (JAMES) *The Red Heart* (1949).
Indian File 4, WREFORD (JAMES) *Of Time and the Lover* (1950).
Indian File 5, BAILEY (A.G.) *Border River* (1952).
Indian File 6, ANDERSON (PATRICK) *The Colour as Naked* (1953).
Indian File 7, PAGE (P.K.) *The Metal and the Flower* (1954).

Indian File 8, WEBB (PHYLLIS) *Even Your Right Eye* (1956).

Indian File 9, GLASSCO (JOHN) *The Deficit Made Flesh* (1958).

Before dismissing Hoffer's claim as wild-eyed, it is salutary to read through a list of Contact Press authors.

It's a claim well worth thinking about.

Tiny audience and massive subsidy combine to produce conditions inimical to the growth of a literature. Subsidy has distorted natural literary development. A literature has its own natural rate of growth and change. Writing and audience grow together. The infusion into this relationship of hundreds of millions of dollars has not caused the audience to grow much larger than it was in the days when The Ryerson Press printed their chapbooks in runs of 250 or 500. It has, however, encouraged an abnormal growth in the number of writers; over 4000 of them now receive payment for the use of their books in public libraries.

(Or, more accurately, for the *holding* of their books in public libraries; if recompense were doled out on the verifiable basis of circulation, then payments to many authors might be low indeed.)

If literary conditions were in any way normal, many of these writers would not be published at all. Lavish grants blunt the necessary element of competition for both writer and publisher; the writer does not have to compete against other writers and the publisher does not have to compete in the market. Everyone is playing games with someone else's money. Government gold has sapped and trivialized us; vision and passion are being tamed and bureaucratized.

But what does it *really* matter, some might say, if instead of 40 writers there are 4000? The best will surely be recognized. Those who are little better than amateurs will fall by the wayside. And don't we *need* a lot of writers and writing so that out of the fertile ruck a few blooms may rise and grow gorgeous?

The best will indeed be recognized – but by whom? And when?

Often only by a small group of their fellow writers. The spate of books pouring from the subsidized presses makes it increasingly difficult to discriminate. Our newspapers regularly review the works of the 4000 but for many reviewers a book is a book. Most of our school teachers teach what they are told to teach. Our libraries dutifully purchase the works of the 4000 because they are Canadian, identify them by red maple leaf stickers on the spine, and slap them on the shelves to do their considerable worst to unwary readers. Under such conditions, it is extremely difficult to locate and educate an audience. The inevitable result is a sad *levelling*, a cultural *numbness*.

The dispensing of government largesse to the 4000 is carried out in fair and democratic fashion. The Canada Council likes to see that all the provinces are represented, that English and French are proportionately dealt with, that there is a measure of sexual equality. Grants are reasonably apportioned between Junior and Senior writers.

No one would be outraged or even faintly surprised to hear that the Council planned to give a proportion of grants to those of 'ethnic' origin or to 'visible minorities' or to homosexuals. Indeed, factions within The Writers' Union are already demanding that 50% of all Council grants be given to women.

Many of us have long understood that The Canada Council is the cultural counterpart to Meals on Wheels.

But it is not only our writers who have been co-opted. The State has, in effect, also bought the academic community. University and academic presses in other countries are forced to agonize over their publishing decisions. Because university funds are limited, competition is keen and standards high. In *our* literary culture, grants *pour* from the cornucopia of The Social Sciences and Humanities Research Council of Canada – a division of The Canada Council. Academics are, in effect, being paid by the State to write about the burgeoning literature which the State is also paying for with money from another of its pockets. Academics are beavering away cataloguing this literature, annotating it, analysing it, deconstructing it, and most of the matter of their labours *is all of twenty-five years old!*

This subsidized rush to judgement is going to prove Gadarene. The process has been accelerating over the last ten years. The ink is scarcely dry upon the author's page before one of the critics is measuring the work up for an article in *Canadian Literature* or in *Essays on Canadian Writing.* Such academic busy-work is distorting our literary culture by slowing or preventing the natural shaking down and settling of reputations over years. Hasty judgements and early enthusiasms are fossilized in the growing number of shoddily edited Companions and Encyclopedias and Histories. The young writer who at 40 is rashly proclaimed a Major Canadian Author may be seen at 65 as an Aging Potboiler, but Major he will remain cemented for decades into the works of reference. For how can we explain away the articles in magazines and journals, the Special Issues, the Symposia, the Colloquia, the Profiles, the explication of the master's *oeuvre* in the Twayne's World Authors Series?

To dismantle all this apparatus would prove too embarrassing.

Because there is no significant audience, our writing has become captive to the academy. Teachers and students at the universities and community colleges *are* the audience. Because there is no Common Reader to exercise the brake of common sense and to assert common experience, there is no one to challenge scholarly pretensions and absurdity. If 'scholarly' is indeed the word ...

The critical reception accorded *In the Village of Viger* illustrates not only the unbridled *arseness* – to use one of Naipaul's Trinidad words – of which literary critics and cultural nationalists are capable but also their irresponsibility towards any relatively sober view of history. It illustrates also what can happen – and what *is* happening – when books are not in the necessary relationship with readers.

LACK OF AUDIENCE is the centre of our problem. Nationalism

is no answer. It has failed in securing an audience in the last sixty years and has failed dismally. The cultural nationalists have attempted to influence the government into Culture by Decree; they have lobbied for subsidy, regulation, and quota. It does not seem to have penetrated with them that culture cannot be imposed.

Before there can be an audience in Canada for Canadian literature there must be an audience for literature; before there can be a love of Canadian literature there must be a general love of writing.

In an essay entitled "The Problem of a Canadian Literature" written in 1943, that robustly sensible critic E.K. Brown wrote:

> The ways of genius cannot be fully predicted; but the "occasional instance," the single man of genius, is not a literature and does not bring a literature into being. No doubt if a Browning or a Yeats were to write in Canada and to make himself felt in Canada, the effect on Canadian literature would be considerable. But the stimulus such a writer could give, great though it would be, and much as it may be wished for by all who hope for the growth of a great literature in this country, would be a passing stimulus, unless it were assisted by social conditions friendly to creative composition. A great literature is the flowering of a great society, a vital and adequate society. Here I must reluctantly take leave of the subject, for it is not in the province of a student of letters to say how a society becomes vital and adequate.

In 1980 I obviously felt confident in going a little further than E.K. Brown. In a talk I gave at the Annual Fall Conference of The Ontario Council of Teachers of English, a talk called "The Yellow School Bus" and subsequently published in *Kicking Against the Pricks*, I said:

> There are good reasons why Canada produces fine hockey players. For each hockey player who achieves national fame,

there are thousands of boys who live and breathe the game, who watch every match, who pore over the hockey cards in bubble gum packets, who play passionately and with burning ambition in streets and alleys until the light fails. And there are mothers and fathers who sanction and foster this ambition, forcing themselves out of bed to drive these boys to practices in the morning dark, forcing themselves out at night to coach and cheer the little leagues.

A great hockey player emerges from *a hockey world.*

All Canadians understand this yet seem puzzled that after pouring good public money down the funnel of The Canada Council they don't seem to be getting Picasso out of the other end.

The simple truth is that just as hockey players are produced from a hockey world, Canadian artists will be, in part, a product of a great Canadian public, a public which is informed, critical, and passionate. Good writing will come from a culture in which native readers, teachers, and students read native writers simply because it is the *normal thing* to read one's own literature.

It is at present rather difficult to read a Canadian book without feeling faintly *virtuous.* Our present "culture" is a subsidized and legislated culture; it must become, however narrowly, a possession of real people....

The idea of a culture, then, does not rest with legislatures, commissions, White Papers, and massive infusions of State cash, but with *you,* with each one of you loving and having faith in something larger and profounder than yourselves. I do not mean that we should become earnest and humourless fanatics. I mean that we should *live* what in our professional lives we profess.

And what, precisely, does *that* mean?

It means that literary taste cannot be separated from the minute and endless activities of our daily lives. What I am trying to say sounds very simple and is not. We read, we understand, we teach what we are. Every time we choose white sliced as opposed to bread, every time we make do with an ugly cup or plate or knife or fork, every time we ignore or are blind to ugliness in our rooms and furnishings, our senses atrophy further and we weaken our ability to share in the visions of those who see more clearly than we do. Every time we accept the convenience of the shoddy, the seeming inevitability of the vulgar, the less able we are to stand up against the values of the market place. If we drink coffee in styrofoam cups from machines, is it not likely that this, and an accumulation of such acts, progressively blunts us? If we do not protest against reconstituted potatoes or frozen french fries, is it really likely that we will protest against imprecise and incorrect language in our newspapers and on the CBC? Would Evelyn Waugh have washed his hair with a shampoo called *Gee, Your Hair Smells Terrific*?

We teach what we are.

I could equally well have said: *We read what we are.*

I WOULD STILL stand by these words and would offer them as a prescription for what we must do and for what we must become if we wish to own a Canadian literature.

And 'Canadian-ness'?

A watched pot, says the proverb, never boils.

A sense of 'Canadian-ness' will inevitably emerge from our literature whether we desire it or not. It was, I believe, Aldous Huxley who once said that happiness cannot be planned and cannot be attained by those consciously seeking it but is rather the unsought by-product of some other activity or concern. When we have stopped obsessively watching Canadian literature's obdurately lukewarm and stodgy pot, a sense of 'Canadian-ness' will one day – like happiness – surprise us.

John Metcalf at Fifty

FICTION

New Canadian Writing, 1969: Stories by John Metcalf, D.O. Spettigue and C.J. Newman. Toronto: Clarke, Irwin, 1969.

The Lady Who Sold Furniture. Toronto: Clarke, Irwin, 1970.

Going Down Slow. Toronto: McClelland and Stewart, 1972.
————. Don Mills, Ont.: PaperJacks, 1975.

The Teeth of My Father. Ottawa: Oberon, 1975.

Metcalf, John, and John Newlove. *Dreams surround us: Fiction and Poetry by John Metcalf & John Newlove.* Delta, Ont.: Bastard, 1977.
"Of this edition of 150 copies 130 are numbered and signed. The remaining 20 copies are for private distribution by the authors." Includes Metcalf's novella "Girl in Gingham" and Newlove's long poem "The Green Plain."

Girl in Gingham. Ottawa: Oberon, 1978.
Republished as *Private Parts: A Memoir.* Scarborough, Ont.: New American Library, 1980.

General Ludd. Downsview, Ont.: ECW, 1980.
————. Toronto: General, 1981.

Selected Stories. New Canadian Library, No. 168. Toronto: McClelland and Stewart, 1982.

Adult Entertainment. Toronto: Macmillan, 1986.

NON-FICTION

Kicking Against the Pricks. Downsview, Ont.: ECW, 1982.
————. 2nd ed. Guelph, Ont.: Red Kite, 1986.

Freedom from Culture. Vancouver: Tanks, 1987.
————. 2nd ed. Pref. William Hoffer. Vancouver: Tanks, 1987.
————. Pref. Walter Block. Vancouver: Fraser Institute, 1988.

What Is A Canadian Literature?. Guelph, Ont.: Red Kite, 1988.

WORKS EDITED AND TEXTBOOKS

Metcalf, John, ed. *The Razor's Edge.* By W. Somerset Maugham. Canadian Educational Edition. Don Mills, Ont.: Bellhaven House, 1967.

Metcalf, John, ed. *The Daughter of Time.* By Josephine Tey. Canadian Educational Edition. Scarborough, Ont.: Bellhaven House, 1968.

Metcalf, John, ed. *Flight of the Phoenix.* By Elleston Trevor. Canadian Educational Edition. Scarborough, Ont.: Bellhaven House, 1968.

Metcalf, John, and Gordon Callaghan. *Rhyme and Reason.* Toronto: Ryerson, 1968.

Rittenhouse, Charles, John Metcalf, and Juliette Dowling. *Wordcraft 2.* Toronto: J.M. Dent, 1968.

Rittenhouse, Charles, John Metcalf, and Juliette Dowling. *Wordcraft 3.* Toronto: J.M. Dent, 1968.

Rittenhouse, Charles, John Metcalf, and Juliette Dowling. *Wordcraft 1.* Toronto: J.M. Dent, 1969.

Metcalf, John, ed. *Sixteen by Twelve: Short Stories by Canadian Writers.* Toronto: Ryerson, 1970.

Metcalf, John, and Gordon Callaghan, eds. *Salutation.* Toronto: Ryerson, 1970.

Rittenhouse, Charles, and John Metcalf. *Wordcraft: Senior*. Toronto: J.M. Dent, 1970.

Metcalf, John, ed. *Kaleidoscope: Canadian Stories*. Photographs by John de Visser. Toronto: Van Nostrand Reinhold, 1972.

Metcalf, John, ed. *The Narrative Voice: Short Stories and Reflections by Canadian Authors*. Toronto: McGraw-Hill Ryerson, 1972.

Metcalf, John, ed. *The Speaking Earth: Canadian Poetry*. Toronto: Van Nostrand Reinhold, 1973.

Harcourt, Joan, and John Metcalf, eds. *76: New Canadian Stories*. Ottawa: Oberon, 1976.

Blaise, Clark, and John Metcalf, eds. *Here & Now: Best Canadian Stories*. Ottawa: Oberon, 1977.

Harcourt, Joan, and John Metcalf, eds. *77: Best Canadian Stories*. Ottawa: Oberon, 1977.

Rittenhouse, Charles, and John Metcalf. *Wordcraft: Junior*. Toronto: J.M. Dent, 1977.

Metcalf, John, and Clark Blaise, eds. *78: Best Canadian Stories*. Ottawa: Oberon, 1978.

Blaise, Clark, and John Metcalf, eds. *79: Best Canadian Stories*. Ottawa: Oberon, 1979.

Metcalf, John, ed. *Stories Plus: Canadian Stories with Authors' Commentaries.* Toronto: McGraw-Hill Ryerson, 1979.

Blaise, Clark, and John Metcalf, eds. *80: Best Canadian Stories.* Ottawa: Oberon, 1980.

Metcalf, John, ed. *First Impressions.* Ottawa: Oberon, 1980.

Metcalf, John, ed. *New Worlds: A Canadian Collection of Stories with Notes.* Toronto: McGraw-Hill Ryerson, 1980.

Metcalf, John, ed. *Second Impressions.* Ottawa: Oberon, 1981.

Metcalf, John, and Leon Rooke, eds. *81: Best Canadian Stories.* Ottawa: Oberon, 1981.

Metcalf, John, ed. *Making It New: Contemporary Canadian Stories.* Toronto: Methuen, 1982.

Metcalf, John, ed. *Third Impressions.* Ottawa: Oberon, 1982.

Metcalf, John, and Leon Rooke, eds. *82: Best Canadian Stories.* Ottawa: Oberon, 1982.

Metcalf, John, and Leon Rooke, eds. *The New Press Anthology: Best Canadian Short Fiction # 1.* New Press Canadian Classics. Toronto: General, 1984.

Metcalf, John, and Leon Rooke, eds. *The New Press Anthology # 2: Best Stories.* New Press Canadian Classics. Toronto: General, 1985.

Metcalf, John, ed. *The Bumper Book.* Toronto: ECW, 1986.

Metcalf, John, ed. *Carry On Bumping.* Toronto: ECW, 1988.

Metcalf, John, ed. *Everyone Leans, Each on Each Other: Words for John Newlove on the Occasion of His Fiftieth Birthday.* Ottawa: Bastard, 1988.
   "Published on Canada Day 1988 by the Bastard Press in an edition of 30 copies."

Metcalf, John, ed. *Writers in Aspic.* Montreal: Véhicule, 1988.

Metcalf, John, and Leon Rooke, eds. *The Macmillan Anthology 1.* Toronto: Macmillan, 1988.

Compiled by J.R. (Tim) Struthers

This printing of *What Is A Canadian Literature?*
is published in an edition of 1250 copies,
1000 of which have been sewn and bound into
paper wraps.

Two hundred and fifty additional copies
have been casebound in cloth, of which thirty
are signed and numbered by the author.

———